THE
LITTLE
BOOK
OF
ANTRIM

BARRY FLYNN

ILLUSTRATED BY
CONOR MCCLURE

To Katrina, Meabh and Deirbhile

First published 2016

The History Press Ireland
50 City Quay
Dublin 2
Ireland
www.thehistorypress.ie

The History Press Ireland are a member of Publishing Ireland,
the Irish Book Publisher's Association.

British Library Cataloguing in Publication Data.
A catalogue record for this book is available from the British Library.

ISBN 978 1 84588 891 6

Typesetting and origination by The History Press
Printed by TJ International Ltd, Padstow, Cornwall

CONTENTS

ACKNOWLEDGEMENT

I would like to thank the Northern Ireland Tourist Board for permission to reproduce a number of its images within this book.

INTRODUCTION

County Antrim is a thing of beauty. From Rathlin Island to the Cave Hill and from the glorious glens to the shores of Lough Neagh, the county is blessed with epic scenery, history and folklore. Scratch the surface and you will find a rich tapestry of stories and this book hopefully has uncovered a hidden tale or two.

Physically Antrim can be breath-taking. At its northern tip lies the UNESCO-recognised world heritage site of the Giant's Causeway. Famously, Dr Samuel Johnson declared that the causeway was, 'Worth seeing, yes; but not worth going to see', yet many tens of thousands of tourists each year would beg to differ.

The famous Antrim Coast Road, built by hand by the 'men of the Glynnes', is considered one of the great tourist routes of the world. Overlooking the road, the nine green glens exude splendour as they sweep down dramatically to the sea.

Inland, Slemish Mountain remains synonymous with St Patrick and the origins of Christianity in Ireland. While despite Antrim's outward beauty, its many castles and forts remind us of a fraught history of warfare and division.

Within the county lies also the world's oldest licenced whiskey distillery, the superb Gobbins Cliff Path and, of course, a large tract of the Victorian city of Belfast. Indeed, did you know that the only bridge to span the Atlantic Ocean can be found at Carrick-a-Rede? It was famously described by William Hamilton as, 'A whimsical little fishing rock, connected to the mainland by a flying bridge.'

At Ballycastle, the Auld Lammas Fair, Ireland's oldest traditional fair, still takes place on the last Monday and Tuesday in August. It is an event celebrated famously in song, while the local delicacies of dulse and 'yella man' still do a roaring trade.

However, this book is also about the people who have brought fame to the county. Antrim has produced men and women who have changed the world; people who have excelled in business, sport, politics, the arts and sciences.

At another level, there are thousands of stories seldom told of people who have contributed to the diverse chronicle of the county. Stories of strange and mysterious occurrences, witchcraft, misfortune, poverty, hunger and skulduggery – some good, some bad and some eye-opening anecdotes in the extreme. There are stories of rebels, rodents, rogues and robbers; chancers, convicts and champions. They have all contributed to the rich tapestry that tells the story of Ireland's green gem of the North East.

1

PEOPLE AND PLACES OF NOTE

LOUGH NEAGH AND RAM'S ISLAND

Lough Neagh washes the shores of Antrim's inner coastline and covers an expanse of 100,000 acres, making it the largest lake in the British Isles. It remains in the ownership of the Earl of Shaftesbury, who, in 2012, indicated that he was hoping to meet with a Stormont working group to assess the possibility of bringing the lough into public ownership. The origin of the lough is surrounded by fable. The most popular of the legends centres around giant Finn McCool, who is said to have lifted a chunk of Ulster and sent it flying into the Irish Sea. The clod became the Isle of Man, while the huge hole left behind became Lough Neagh.

Ram's Island, which lies a mile off the shore near Glenavy, was originally a monastic settlement and its ruined tower is testament to that period. The tower itself is just over 40ft high and is similar to those found throughout Ireland. In the winter of 1879, Charles Kingsley, the distinguished naturalist and author of *The Water Babies*, visited the island. His visit coincided with one of the coldest winters on record and he was able to skate across the lough to Ram's Island. He recalled, 'Ram's Island reached and the round tower explored, we returned again to the Antrim shore, where games of various kinds and skating were indulged.' It is believed that 1879 was the third time during that century that the lough had frozen over.

During Victorian times, a summer house was constructed by Lord O'Neill and was set in an exotic garden. During the Second World War, the island was a favourite haunt for soldiers of the US Army at Langford Lodge. However, vandalism was rife and one night during the war arsonists visited the island and burned down the summer house.

HILDEN'S WORLD-FAMOUS THREAD MILL

The world-renowned Barbour linen thread works were established in Lisburn in 1784 by John Barbour, who was originally from Scotland. In 1817, his son, William, bought a bleaching green at nearby Hilden and the workforce expanded rapidly. The family built a model village for the workers, which consisted of 350 houses, two schools, a community hall and a village sports ground. However, despite its tranquil setting on the banks of the River Lagan, all was not as peaceful as it seemed.

The arrival of a strolling fiddler in Hilden on Monday 10 August 1858 was to have devastating consequences for local millworkers Owen Hughes and James Kelly. Being in a cheerful mood, the two men asked the fiddler to perform at a local house and the musical entertainment lasted until eleven that evening when two neighbours, father and son, John and Alexander Martin, arrived to complain about the noise. On threatening to fetch Mr Barbour, the mill owner, a fight ensued in the street during which Hughes and Kelly were stabbed and died. At court, Alexander Martin was found guilty of manslaughter, while his father John was acquitted.

THE 'FORT OF THE GAMBLERS'

The town of Lisburn, together with Newry, was afforded city status in 2002 by Queen Elizabeth II as part of her Golden Jubilee celebrations. Lisburn's name derives from the Irish *Lios na gCearrbhach*, meaning 'ring fort of the gamblers'. It became known as Lisnagarvey, and eventually Lisburn. The original ring fort of the gamblers was thought to have been located on the northern side of the city's Wallace Park. The name Lisnagarvey is preserved in the name of the local hockey club and high school.

ARMOY ROUND TOWER

A classic example of an Irish round tower is situated in Armoy, 6 miles south of Ballycastle, and dates back to the eleventh century when Viking raids were frequent in the area. Its door, at 5ft 9in high

and merely 19in wide, is claimed to be the narrowest round-tower door in Ireland. It stands 5ft off the ground, but would have been higher when constructed since the surrounding land has 'risen' due to the thousands of burials that have taken place in the adjoining graveyard. The tower was excavated in the 1840s by Edmund Getty, who discovered a skull still attached to its spinal column, which is thought to have belonged to an ancient chieftain killed in battle. The tower today is a ruined stump, standing currently at 36ft in height; the original tower was estimated to have been over 60ft high. In 1997, excavations under the existing church uncovered the feet of a medieval leper – he must have been a powerful figure since he was permitted a burial on consecrated land. The neighbouring St Patrick's Church of Ireland parish church was built in 1820 and is on the site of the original church founded in AD 460 by St Olcan, a disciple of Patrick.

DR GRAHAM'S LUNATIC ASYLUM

In December 1825, an advertisement appeared in the *Belfast News Letter* seeking a site for the Antrim and Down Lunatic Asylum. The advert stressed that the grounds 'should be within a mile of Belfast, not containing less than six acres, and having the command of a plentiful supply of spring water'. Within a year, the Commissioners of Lunatic Asylums in Ireland had secured a site which was formerly the home of Joseph Stevenson at Springfield, on the Falls Road in Belfast. The site, which was at the junction of the modern-day Falls and Grosvenor roads, was opened in May 1829. A notice appeared in local papers informing that, 'The Directors will consider applications for admission on the first Monday of every month by form of application which may be had from the Manager, Mr Cummings, either personally any day, between the hours of ten and four o'clock, or by letter, post-paid'. The entry criteria was quite strict, confining admissions to those cases which come strictly under the denomination of 'lunatics or the class of idiots', with persons suffering from epilepsy 'under no circumstances being received'.

By the late 1890s, the asylum had become known as 'Graham's Home', named after Dr William Graham, who was superintendent at the facility during that period. Graham had studied mental health in London and in 1896 he succeeded Dr Merrick as resident medical superintendent. He developed a humanitarian reputation as a man who had deep sympathy for his patients. Graham was obliged to present a yearly report on the asylum which was published in most of the Irish daily papers. In local folklore in Belfast, the name of 'Graham's Home' is immortalised in the phrase uttered by many a distressed mother to her troublesome children: 'You'll have me ready for Graham's home.'

The home was succeeded by a newer development on the outskirts of south Belfast at Purdysburn, while the site of 'Graham's Home' is now incorporated within the Royal Victoria Hospital. In 1949, the estate known as The Abbey, Muckamore, near Antrim town, was purchased by the Northern Ireland Hospitals' Authority for use as a 'colony for treatment of mentally-retarded persons'. Over the next twenty years, over £1 million was spent developing the settlement, which had room for 1,000 persons. Planned on the 'villa' system, Muckamore contained a farm, workshops and a cinema.

KILLEAD'S APACHE HUNTER

Born in Killead in 1793, James Kirker emigrated from Ireland to New York in 1810 and soon found work as a fur trader in New Mexico. Despite working closely with members of the local Apache tribe, he took up a position as a bounty hunter with the Mexican government, who employed him to track down members of the Apache tribe who were involved in cattle raids. Kirker led a paramilitary force with gusto against the 'troublesome' Apaches during the mid-1840s and claimed the scalps of 500 warriors at a dividend of $200 a head – the bounty for a woman's scalp was $50 and for a child's scalp it was $25.

BILLY THE KID – ALIAS 'KID ANTRIM'

Apart from the infamous nickname 'Billy the Kid', William H. Bonney was known as Henry McCarty and by the nickname 'Kid Antrim'. His mother, Catherine McCarty, was born in County Antrim in 1829 and emigrated to New York during the Great Famine in 1846. In the United States, she married William Harrison Bonney and 'The Kid' was born in New York in 1859. Billy's natural father died in 1862 and his mother then moved to New Mexico where, ironically, she married a William Antrim.

TEMPLEPATRICK'S CYCLING STAR

The name Edward 'Teddy' Hale may not be widely remembered in the cycling world, but in 1896 he was simply untouchable in the sport. That year he won the world-famous 'Garden Six' endurance race in New York, which was considered at that time to be the toughest endurance race in the world. Said to have been born in Templepatrick in 1864, Hale, who competed for the Lainsborough Bicycle Club, had become the unofficial European champion earlier that year when he won the Continental Endurance Race in Berlin. He was then invited to enter the world-famous American Madison Square Garden six-day cycle race in December 1896.

The race, which took place between 7 and 13 December, saw the cream of world cycling battle it out for the ultimate prize in the sport, with the winner being the rider who covered the longest distance over the oval course. At 10 p.m. on 13 December, as the band struck up 'The Wearin' of the Green', 10,000 spectators cheered wildly as Hale was declared the winner, having completed 1,911 miles over the course. He had beaten the runner-up, Albert Schock of the United States, by over 300 miles and claimed the $1,300 prize with ease. The race itself was characterised by riders pushing themselves to the limit, often suffering from hallucinations and delusions. Hale, who had smoked countless cigarettes throughout the event to relieve the boredom, was feted for his achievements by many Irish-American societies. He continued to compete in endurance races, but his physical exertions were thought to have contributed to his untimely death at the age of 47 in 1911.

KENNETH MCARTHUR – HERO FROM DERVOCK

Born in County Antrim in 1881, Kennedy Kane (Kenneth) McArthur's greatest sporting triumph came on 14 July 1912, when he won gold in the marathon at the Stockholm Olympic Games. He grew up in Dervock and attended the local national school before becoming a postman, known affectionately in the area as 'Big Ken'. In 1899, he joined the Irish Rifles and served in South Africa and, after the Boer War, decided to stay, joining the Baden Powell police constabulary.

Standing at 6ft 3in, McArthur took up running at a late age and became a successful cross-country competitor, being chosen to represent South Africa at the 1912 Olympics. The marathon that year was run in sweltering conditions, but the big Antrim man took the lead towards the end of the race and beat his fellow countryman Christian Gitsham for the gold medal. As he ran towards the finishing line, a northern accent in the crowd was said to have shouted, 'Come on, Antrim! Come on, ye boy ye!'

On his way back to South Africa, McArthur stopped off to see his father at Dervock, where huge crowds gathered to salute their hero. In Ballymoney, he was carried on the shoulders of the crowd to the town hall where a large bronze plaque was unveiled in McArthur's honour. He was an exceptional character, who battled constantly against weight problems and had a love of pipe-smoking. He died in South Africa in June 1960 and his name is preserved by the athletics stadium in the town of Potchefstroom.

In his honour, the Olympic torch was paraded through Dervock in 2012 in the run-up to the London Olympic Games. A blue plaque was erected in his memory by the Ulster History Circle in Dervock in 2011.

PADDY BREAKS
THE CYCLING RECORD

The month of August 1952 was one of the wettest on record. However, the inclement weather did not deter Ballycastle cyclist Paddy McNeilly from breaking an Irish record by cycling from Mizen Head in Cork to Ballycastle in 21 hours, 2 minutes and 30 seconds. The plumber set off on the 384-mile journey on the afternoon of 16 August and rode through a stormy night to break the previous record by 1 hour and 12 minutes. Cheered on by crowds along the way, 33-year-old Paddy was even afforded free passage by customs men who shouted encouragement as he crossed the border near Newry. He arrived in Ballycastle on Sunday afternoon. Hundreds of locals and holidaymakers greeted him with roars of approval. One observer noted when Paddy's new record time was declared, 'Why that is faster than we could have come by train.'

CHARLESTOWN HIBERNIAN HALL

A little piece of County Antrim is preserved outside the Hibernian Hall in Charlestown, South Carolina, where a pillar from the Giant's Causeway greets visitors. The pillar was brought to Charlestown in 1851 and sits behind the fence on the porch and is inscribed, 'A section from one of the pillars of the Giants Causeway, County Antrim, Ireland – 1851'. The hall was built in 1801 and contains a panel adorned with a harp over its doorway. The Hibernian Society of Charlestown is still active and meets regularly, electing a president every two years, alternating between a representative of the city's Catholic and Protestant residents.

2

STRANGE HAPPENINGS
IN COUNTY ANTRIM

THE CRUMLIN METEORITE – 1902

Situated 12 miles to the west of Belfast, the relative tranquillity
of the town of Crumlin was disturbed on the morning of
13 September 1902, when a large meteorite landed on the farm of
Mr William Walker.

Situated at Crosshill to the north of the town, Walker's farmhands
were reaping the harvest when a loud explosion occurred 20 yards
from where John Adams was picking apples. The noise of the
explosion was heard 13 miles away in Lurgan. Adams, after
composing himself, no doubt, began digging out the large smoking
and hissing stone, which had embedded itself a foot deep in the
soil. The 9.5lb meteorite was still warm an hour after it had been
recovered and was described as being the size of a football. It was the
largest meteorite to have fallen on the British Isles since 1795. Most
of its associated debris is believed to have landed in nearby Lough
Neagh. A resident of the village, Mrs Ethel Walker, told the press
that the noise the meteorite had created on landing persuaded many
locals that 'Judgement Day' had arrived. The meteorite soon came
to the attention of collectors and, despite being keen to hold onto the
artefact, William Walker was persuaded to sell it to Mr L. Fletcher of
the British Natural History Museum and it has been on exhibition
since then, in its central hall in London.

UNPRODUCTIVE SEARCH FOR THE JEWELS OF AN EMPEROR

Treasure-hunting expeditions do not spring to mind when considering the coastal town of Cushendall. However, in 1933, six men from the area set sail as part of an expedition on the *Salvor* in an attempt to find the missing ship, the *Merida*, which lay 200ft underwater 60 miles off Cape Charles, Virginia. The ship sank in 1911, with a loss of $2 million worth of Mexican gold, silver, copper and the jewels of the Emperor Maximilian and Empress Carlotta of Mexico. The crew of the *Salvor* had invested their life savings to be part of the expedition; they had been promised a twentyfold return should the treasure be recovered. The County Antrim men were Malcolm and Charles McCambridge, John McElheron, John and James McKeegan, all from Cushendall, and John Hyndman from Glenariffe.

The search for the lost ship began in late 1932 under the command of Captain Harry L. Bowdein, who had secured financial backing for his project from Wall Street bankers, including Percy Rockefeller and Vincent Astor. Owing to the risk of attack by pirates, the crew were heavily armed and prohibited from writing detailed letters home. Hopes were high that the treasure had been found and, in August 1933, it was reported that the ship's safe had been uncovered. However, nothing was found and the expedition ended in failure. The men returned to a humble life in the Glens in November, with their dreams of riches shattered. It was discovered that the ship had already been plundered and the journey had been in vain.

A HIGH-SOCIETY SCANDAL

The whiff of high-society scandal was in the air at the Dundarave Estate, near Bushmills, in December 1882, when Sir Francis Edmund Workman Macnaghten filed for divorce due to his wife's infidelity. Sir Francis, 3rd Baronet and Chief of the Clan Macnaghten, was a Conservative-Unionist politician with a fine military career. He had married Alice Mary Russell in 1868 and they had four children. Lady Macnaghten was twenty years her husband's junior and they were very much part of the Irish aristocracy. Their marriage was an unhappy one.

In December 1882, Sir Frederick arrived home early from a shooting expedition to discover that a local land agent, Frederick Thornhill, was present in his wife's bedroom. A row ensued and Macnaghten ordered Thornhill to leave the house, only for Lady Macnaghten to beg her husband to let him stay for dinner; otherwise the servants would 'gossip'. Sir Francis relented, but the following day he returned home to find that he wife had left for Dublin with Thornhill. Travelling post-haste to Dublin, Francis traced the couple a week later to the Royal Hotel in Bray. He begged his wife to come home. However, she was not keen on reconciliation and refused to read letters he had brought from her children begging her to return. The divorce case was heard at the High Court in London in February 1883, where Sir Francis was granted a decree nisi due to his wife's infidelity – or, as it was reported in the papers, 'her misconduct'.

ANTRIM TOWN LEFT WITHOUT WATER

While August 1952 was one of the wettest in recent decades, July that year was one of the driest. In Antrim town, the 15-million-gallon-capacity reservoir which supplied the town ran dry for the first time in living memory. A majority of houses were left without water, forcing men and women to queue with buckets at the pumps. Not even the oldest inhabitant could remember the last such shortage. The irony of the situation, of course, was that the town lay less than 2 miles from Lough Neagh, the largest expanse of fresh water in the British Isles. Hasty arrangements were made by Antrim Rural Council and the Ministry of Health to connect a pipe from the lough to a main to alleviate the situation.

DID NAZI BOMBERS VISIT ANTRIM?

Belfast was the subject of a devastating Nazi bombing blitz in April and May 1941, but there is also evidence that German bombs fell over County Antrim during March that year. On the nights of 13 and 14 March 1941, German bombers, which had travelled from northern France up the Irish Sea to Scotland, attacked the factories and shipyards of Clydeside. Approximately 270 bombers were involved in the raids, dropping high explosives, incendiary bombs and landmines over a nine-hour period during which 528 people were killed.

The firestorm created was visible over large areas of north Antrim and as the bombers escaped they jettisoned munitions over a wide area. On 14 March, three children, James Turner, Ivan and Claire Milliken, were injured at Ballyduff, near Glengormley. It is believed that one of them disturbed a bomb that had been lying in a field, causing it to explode. After receiving medical attention, they were removed to the Belfast Children's Hospital.

Three bombs fell in Aghagallon and were discovered close to a farm and subsequently removed by a British Air Force bomb disposal unit. Two other bombs that fell in a field within a mile radius exploded, leaving cavities of about 3ft in diameter in each case.

ANTRIM MAN ANNOUNCES DISCOVERY OF PLUTO

County Antrim-born astronomer, Dr Andrew Crommelin, a descendant of Louis de Crommelin of Lisburn linen fame, was noted as the man who announced to the world the discovery of Pluto in 1930. The Cushendall native, who was of Huguenot stock and a former president of the Royal Astronomical Society, published an article which claimed that a celestial body first noticed by Belgian astronomers was not a comet, but in fact a planet. The Crommelin name is commemorated in the village of Newtown Crommelin, 8 miles from Ballymena, work on which was commenced in 1824 by Nicholas Crommelin.

While many believe that Pluto was named after Goofy's pet dog, it was, in fact, named after the Roman god of the underworld. Crommelin's claim to have discovered a 'planet' was rebutted in 2006, when Pluto was re-classified to 'dwarf-planet' status by the International Astronomical Union.

OUTRAGE IN A
PORTGLENONE GRAVEYARD

The easing of the Penal Laws in Ireland enabled Catholics to lease land, build churches and establish their own graveyards. In 1774, Father John Cassidy, parish priest of Ahoghill and Portglenone, acquired property at Aughnahoy for that purpose and was buried there in early January 1819. However, his grave was disturbed in one of the most shocking acts ever witnessed in County Antrim. The outrageous action was even more peculiar as, despite the fact that grave robbing was rife in the Ireland at that time, no attempt was made to steal the body. The sight which greeted Father Peter McNally, the newly installed parish priest, in the graveyard on the morning of 19 January was truly horrific. Such was the outrage that the following notice was published in the *Belfast News Letter* in February and March 1819. Despite the appeal, the graveyard ghouls were never apprehended:

OUTRAGE AND REWARD

WHEREAS the GRAVE YARD of AUGHNAHOY, near PORTGLENONE in the County of Antrim, was Entered on the night of MONDAY the 18th of January last, and the GRAVE of the late Rev. JOHN CASSIDY, Parish Priest of AHOGHILL, was Opened, the Coffin broken, and the Body stripped of part of its covering. Now we, whose Names are hereunto subscribed, holding in merited abhorrence and act so barbarous and inhuman, do promise to pay, in proportion to the several sums to our names annexed, ONE HUNDRED POUNDS STERLING, To any Person who, within Six Months, will discover, and prosecute to conviction, the Person or Persons guilty of said offence; and we promise to pay the Sum of THIRTY POUNDS STERLING, for such information as may lead to the discovery of the Person or Persons guilty of this shameful and un-Christian act.

CRUMLIN'S ANNUAL RAT RACE

The 'sport' of rat racing thrived on the shores of Lough Neagh in the 1960s, with the annual championships taking place in Norman Wilson's bar in the main street of Crumlin. The contestants raced each other through transparent plastic tubes, 25ft long, which were suspended from the ceiling. In 1968, the champion rodent, which hailed from Donaghadee, County Down, clocked a time of 12.4 seconds. However, the 'track record' was held by a local rat, Aghadalgan Bill, who had completed the course in 10 seconds. Speaking to local reporters, Mr Wilson explained that upwards of £18 had been paid for a thoroughbred rat. 'Sometimes they bite, but usually they are attended at races by experienced handlers,' explained Wilson. 'On occasions a temperamental competitor refuses to run and sits down to lick its face, which means disqualification.' First prize in the annual championship was the curiously named Rhubarb Cup, which had been the trophy presented to the winner of the defunct rhubarb section of the yearly Crumlin Agricultural Show. 'Instead of letting the cup go to waste,' explained Mr Wilson, 'we decided to present it to the winning owner in the rat racing championship.'

THE ANTRIM VOLCANO 'MYSTERY'

Standing at almost 1,700ft, Knocklayd Mountain overlooks the town of Ballycastle and affords a picturesque view of the Scottish Lowlands. Crowned by the ancient monument Carn na Truagh (the cairn of sorrow), the mountain was the scene for one of Ireland's most spectacular (and disputed) geographical events in May 1788. On the day in question, it was said that the mountain erupted, 'sending a column of fire 60 yards into the air'. The surrounding area was showered with ash and stones and this was followed by a stream of 'lava', which destroyed the nearby (but seemingly fictitious) village of Ballyowen. It was said that the lava flowed across the area for the following two days. The 'eruption' of Knocklayd was said to have been foretold by the Julia McQuillen, the 'Black Nun' of nearby Bonamargy Friary, who prophesied in the seventeenth century that the mountain would explode and cover the surrounding area in raging fires. News of the event was reported in a letter in the *Dublin*

Chronicle of 7 June 1788; however, the letter was dismissed as a 'narrative that was fabulous'. The event was referred to by William Beggs in his 1820 poem 'Rathlin', but very little contemporary evidence exists. Geologists, however, have since suggested that the event could have occurred due to a massive bog slide on the mountain that ignited the coal seam which runs from Fair Head to the mountain.

VIOLENT TREMORS HIT BALLYCLARE

Residents of Ballyclare were thrown into a panic on the morning of Wednesday 25 May 1910, when violent earth tremors struck the town from 8 a.m. The stillness of the area was interrupted as underground tremors shook windows and doors, sending dogs sprinting to their kennels in apparent terror. People, although not in a state of wild panic, gathered in the streets as plates smashed on kitchen floors and windowpanes shattered. The tremors lasted until midday and further disturbances were reported in the town of Newtownards, County Down. Despite there being no obvious cause, the *Belfast Telegraph* suggested that the shocks were due to artillery practice at Greypoint, near Crawfordsburn, on the shores of Belfast Lough.

PORTGLENONE VISITED BY ALIENS?

The phenomena of a UFO 'sighting' caused great excitement in Portglenone in 1958. Local farmer Joseph Bennett claimed that he witnessed an object swoop down on a field and cut an oak tree in two. The object, he said, was about 7ft wide and was hovering in the air like 'a great rushing wind' when it suddenly swooped down and cut through the trunk of the tree without pausing. Dr E. Lindsay, director of the Armagh Observatory, said that what Mr Bennett saw was consistent with a whirlpool, or miniature tornado, which been witnessed in the Armagh area in recent years. He discounted the theory that it might have been a meteor, which, he pointed out, was usually accompanied by a bright glow.

In Glenarm, in 1967, residents were perplexed when a 'small red-hot object' landed in the village on the night of Thursday 15 June. Mrs Nell McAllister was awoken with a jolt when a mystery object crashed onto her roof. Upon hurrying outside with her elderly mother, she found a glowing piece of metal 'shaped like a pudding basin' lying on the ground. Police were alerted to the incident and after making enquiries it was established that the object had not fallen off a spaceship; rather it was the remains of a buoy which had exploded when a local fisherman had tried to open it with a blow torch. With calm restored to the village, Mrs McAllister and her shaken mother returned home, happy in the knowledge that aliens had not landed in Glenarm.

THE DOCTOR WITH THE 'CURE FOR CANCER'

With medical science still battling to find a cure for cancer, it is reassuring to know that in 1829 David Reid, from Ballymoney, felt it necessary to tell the world of his 'miracle cure' at the hands of the Belfast physician, Doctor Broom. Taking out a full-page advertisement in the *News Letter* of 3 February, Reid advised readers that he had been afflicted by a cancer on his upper lip for fourteen years. All sorts of cures had been tried, including mercury, cutting, burning, ointments and potions, to no avail. That was until Reid was approached by 'a pleasant young gentleman' who advised him that 'Doctor Broom is the only man on this earth who can cure that dreadful disease'. On travelling to Belfast, he placed himself under the care of Dr Broom and, sure enough, an astonishing and complete cure was effected within weeks. 'The truth is what is here stated,' added Reid, who ended his testimony by declaring it in the name 'of God and the world'. The article ended coincidentally with details of Dr Broom's surgery in Great George's Street in Belfast; a man, it stated, who was also proficient in the cure of the 'King's Evil' and the only man in the world capable of ridding patients of the disease.

THE QUACK DOCTOR OF OLD BELFAST

At the Belfast quarter sessions on 20 January 1876, a Mr James Graham was sentenced to twelve months' hard labour for 'representing himself to the public as a medical practitioner, he being unqualified'. Graham was accused of 'going among the working classes of the town imposing upon them worthless medicines', claiming to be a specialist in the treatment of a disease called 'Wolf of the Liver'. Graham had arrived in Belfast with a plethora of 'medical certificates' and had proceeded through the town with a placard claiming he had cures for all aches, pains and illnesses. On treating a patient, he would advise them that their recovery would be rapid once they took his pills and that he would return two days hence to check on their progress. However, with money in hand, Graham swiftly left his patients' houses, never to be seen again. The judge took a dim view of Graham's antics, telling him he had 'extracted money from the poor of Belfast by pretending to treat diseases of which he was totally ignorant'. He added that he would not tolerate quack doctors who traded on the 'gullibility of the poor' and sentenced him to five years' imprisonment.

WAR ON FOXES IN THE GLENS

The battle between farmers and foxes in County Antrim has been a long and bloody affair. In the 1920s, the number of foxes in the Glens of Antrim increased greatly, forcing farmers to hire the services of Murdo Monro, an expert trapper from the Scottish Highlands. Monro waged an intensive war in the hills and trapped over 140 foxes over a twelve-month period. 'I have cleared out dens,' said Munro, 'that were simply littered with the remains of lambs, grouse, hares, rabbits and farm poultry.' In 1934, the grouse-hunting season in the Ballycastle area was threatened by the work of foxes in the hills. In the five and a half years from January 1945 to July 1950, specialist hunters killed 7,028 foxes in Antrim. In the 1950s, questions were asked on the floor of Stormont about the problem. Farmers were forced to organise a dedicated hunt throughout the district and employ five full-time trappers, paying them £3 10*s* a week.

RABBITS RAVAGE THE GLENDU GLEN

Despite the prevalence of foxes in the Antrim Glens, in August 1933 hordes of rabbits living in burrows on the slopes of Glendu Glen, near Cushendall, almost wiped out the crop of oats, cabbage and turnips. In Cushleake, between Cushendun and Torr Head, rabbits caused thousands of pounds worth of damage as an explosion of their population saw crops ravaged. Police reported that 'no amount of trapping, shooting, or hunting seems to check the damage'. Sergeant Connell of the RUC in Cushendall reported that when on duty in Glendun Glen he saw a field of oats 'move as if alive with rabbits'. Farmers appealed to the Ministry of Agriculture's scientific research department to see if it was possible to fight the animals by introducing disease into their burrows.

BIZARRE ITEMS FOUND IN THE 'DEVIL'S HIDEOUT'

Fears that witchcraft had made a reappearance in the Islandmagee area surfaced in October 1961, when a number of mysterious items were discovered at the 'Devil's Hideout' at the Gobbins cliffs. Five boys from Belfast had been cycling in the area when one discovered a cardboard box hidden in the cave. Inside were black candles, wine glasses, black hoods and cloaks, a chalice and a wooden carving of a serpent's head. Police were called to the scene and took the box away to be examined, stating that they believed they had foiled a 'Black Mass'. It was claimed by locals that an organisation known as 'The Brotherhood of the Left Hand' had been active in the south-east Antrim area. Others, though, felt that it had been an elaborate hoax to coincide with the Halloween period.

THE 'CHILD-EATING' STOAT MYSTERY

In July 1911, the *Northern Whig*'s 'Nature Notes' correspondence had the unenviable task of relating an incident that sent shock waves through Antrim. The story concerned a lady who had travelled from Belfast with her child and the child's nursemaid to holiday at Whitehead in a remote cottage. One fine morning, the nursemaid left the child in its pram outside the cottage to take in the sea air and went to the kitchen to carry out her chores. On returning, she saw what she took to be a rat jump from the pram and scurry off into a nearby hedge. In a panic, she ran to the child, who was lifeless and bleeding profusely from a deep wound on its left wrist. A doctor was called post-haste and a blood transfusion was hastily administered, saving the child's life. On further examination it was determined that the 'rat' was in fact a stoat, which were known to be rampant in the area. The incident resulted in calls for a cull of stoats in Antrim, while others argued that such a step would result in an increase in the number of rats and rabbits in the vicinity. The correspondent concluded that the incident should 'act as a warning to mothers of young children, not to leave them unattended, especially in rural areas'.

THE HUNGRY FERRET
OF AUGHTERDONEY

The ability of rodents to cause physical injuries to humans in Antrim again came to prominence in December 1927. Patrick McKeown, a resident of Aughterdoney, near Ahoghill, was sleeping soundly in his bed when he was attacked by his own ferret, which had escaped from its box, which was kept in the garden of McKeown's house. The animal made its way inside the house and attacked its owner, eating one of the unfortunate man's eyes, while his other eye was severely damaged. When a neighbour, Daniel Warden, arrived at the house on hearing screams, he too was attacked by the ferret and had his hands severely cut. Medics were called and an unconscious McKeown was rushed to hospital in Ballymena. The animal was, needless to say, destroyed.

3

POLITICS, SKULDUGGERY AND INTRIGUE

FACTION FIGHT IN PORTRUSH

Yesterday afternoon a faction fight took place in Portrush, County Antrim, between a Roman Catholic party and an Orange band of excursionists. The police charged and dispersed the opposing mobs, and effected several arrests. Stone-throwing was freely indulged in, and several persons from both sides were seriously injured.

(*The Press Association*, Tuesday 26 June 1883)

SUFFRAGIST ATTACKS IN EAST ANTRIM

In 1914, with Ireland on the brink of civil war over the Home Rule Crisis, violence associated with the campaign for women's suffrage broke out in County Antrim. In 1913, Sir Edward Carson had pledged that women would be permitted voting rights in the Unionist-inspired 'Provisional Government of Ulster', which he had proposed in opposition to Home Rule. However, Carson was a conservative at heart when it came to women's rights and it soon became obvious that he would not honour that pledge. In early March 1914, members of the Belfast branch of the Women's Social and Political Branch (WSPB) besieged Carson's London home, for nearly five days before he agreed to meet with them. When he refused to guarantee the rights of Ulster women in the new political system, Dorothy Evans, the leader of the Belfast branch, ended the truce by stating, 'Carson was no friend of women and we're declaring war on him.' Indicating that the suffragettes were intending to resort to violence, Irish suffragette leader Hannah Sheehy Skeffington wrote, 'women have been harried and persecuted, imprisoned and tortured for acts not one quarter so criminal and threatening to the good order of the community as those of Sir Edward Carson's armed following.'

The 'war' on Carson soon began with an attack on 27 March 1914 on Abbeylands, the home of Major General Sir Hugh McCalmot, a staunch supporter of Carson who had permitted the Ulster Volunteer Force to drill in the grounds of the house. The house, described as a 'splendid country residence' and situated close to Whiteabbey, was destroyed in the fire, despite the best attempts of local men to quench the flames. Two weeks later, on 9 April, Orlands, a large unoccupied mansion near Carrickfergus, which had been purchased by the Catholic Church, was burned to the ground. On examination by the police, a large amount of suffragist literature was discovered in the grounds which stated, 'Apply to Sir Edward Carson for damages – in reply to Carson's betrayal to Irish women' and 'Sir Edward Carson threatens to destroy life – Women only destroy property'. Another postcard read, 'Carson talks; Redmond talks – Suffragettes act. – apply to Carson for compensation.'

Unionist revulsion at the action of the women's rights activists was demonstrated in an incident which occurred in Ballymena in July 1914. Two Austrian ladies on a motoring tour of Ireland were mistaken by a crowd for suffragettes. They were surrounded by a hostile mob, which shouted anti-suffragist abuse at them. Forced to take refuge in a shop, they were eventually rescued by the local UVF commander, who escorted them to their hotel.

'UNSWERVING LOYALTY TO THE KING': REACTION IN ANTRIM TO EASTER 1916

The events in Dublin during Easter week in 1916 were not well received by the great and the good in County Antrim. The board of the Presbyterian Church discussed the Rising at its meeting in Belfast on 2 May and expressed 'its deepest shame' at the actions of the rebels. In passing a resolution condemning the uprising, the Board said 'that Ireland had been humiliated by their [the rebels'] actions before the world'. Sympathy was also in short supply at the meeting of Antrim County Council that day, when councillors passed a motion which 'regarded with detestation the recent attempt, most happily frustrated, of a small section of the Irish people to aid the enemies of the empire by open rebellion, and take this opportunity of proclaiming on behalf of our prosperous county our unswerving devotion and loyalty to our king'.

AN UNUSUAL INCIDENT OF POLITICAL HARMONY

Sometimes in County Antrim, religious and political differences have been set aside for mutual celebrations. Take this example from March 1928, when an Armoy boy was acquitted at the Ballycastle petty sessions of damaging a gate with a stone in his home village. Whatever the circumstances, the news was greeted by an impromptu 'victory' parade in Armoy during which a Hibernian and Orange band played alternatively 'The Boyne Water' and 'The Boys of Wexford', while a bonfire blazed for hours in the street.

THE INSURRECTION OF WILLIAM ORR

In September 1796, a young Antrim farmer named William Orr was arrested and taken to Carrickfergus prison, where he was kept for twelve months without being charged. A year later he was placed in the dock and charged with 'administering the oath of the United Irishmen to soldiers whilst they were still wearing the King's uniform'. Orr was the first to be charged under the Insurrection Act of 1796. He had been betrayed by two soldiers who told the authorities that Orr would be returning to the family home in Farranshane, where his father lay dying. The house was raided and Orr was discovered in an oat bin in an outhouse.

Born in 1766, Orr was a farmer and the son of a highly respected owner of a bleaching green. Fully 6ft in height, he was striking, well-proportioned and of commanding presence. It was suggested by the prosecution that he was attempting to seduce the soldiers from their allegiance to the king and to get them to revolt against 'lawful authority'. He was found guilty and, in what was seen as a pre-emptive strike against the United Irishmen, sentenced to death. He was hanged in Carrickfergus on Saturday, 14 October 1797. His final words from the scaffold were, 'I am no traitor! I am persecuted for my country. I die in the true faith of a Presbyterian.'

THE CROSS OF RODDY MCCORLEY

On 1 January 1969, a cross commemorating the 1798 patriot Roddy McCorley was damaged in a bomb attack by Loyalists in the town of Toomebridge. The attack coincided with a rise in community strife associated with the four-day march from Belfast to Derry by members of the nationalist People's Democracy movement. The incident was described as 'an outrageous affair' by Kevin Agnew, a Maghera solicitor, who was the Republican candidate in the forthcoming Mid-Ulster by-election. It is thought that those responsible for the incident took advantage of the fact that all available RUC officers in the area had been deployed 8 miles away at Randalstown, protecting the marchers, who were billeted in a Hibernian Hall at the end of the first day of their 73-mile trek to Derry from Belfast.

The monument was less than 50 yards from the back door of the RUC station. No windows were broken in houses in the vicinity of the explosion. The memorial stood on the banks of the River Bann on the spot where 19-year-old McCorley had been hanged for his role in the 1798 Rebellion. It was located a short distance from the road bridge connecting counties Antrim and Derry and had been given a 'facelift' in 1966 in time for the 1916 Easter Rising jubilee commemoration ceremonies which took place in the village.

Born to a Presbyterian family in the townland of Duneane, Roddy McCorley's father had been deported to Botany Bay for stealing sheep and for making pikes. McCorley had gone on the run after the 1798 Rebellion and was arrested and sentenced to death after a trial in Ballymena. McCorley was hanged from makeshift gallows on the bridge at Toome on 28 February 1800. Afterwards, his body was disembowelled and his remains buried at the site of his execution. In 1852, a relative had the body reinterred in the Presbyterian graveyard in Duneane. The Celtic cross in memory of McCorley was erected in Toome in 1904 at a cost of £335. After it was damaged in 1969, it lay adjacent to the RUC station in the town until 2001, when it was repaired and donated to the Roddy McCorley Society in Andersonstown. McCorley was commemorated in song by Ethna Carbery in 1904.

HENRY JOY McCRACKEN

Born on 31 August 1767, at 39 High Street, Belfast, Henry Joy McCracken was one of the founders of the United Irishmen and became one of the society's leaders in Antrim and Ulster. He was born into a prominent Presbyterian family as the fifth son of Captain John McCracken, a Belfast ship-owner, and Ann Joy, daughter of Francis Joy, who had founded the *Belfast News Letter* in 1737. By 1791, McCracken had been radicalised by the prevailing revolutionary politics of the time and had been greatly impressed by the message of Thomas Paine's *The Rights of Man*. He forged links with Thomas Russell, Theobald Wolfe Tone and Samuel Neilson and was instrumental in the founding of the Society of United Irishmen on 14 October 1791. In June 1795, McCracken, together with Wolfe Tone, Samuel Neilson, Robert Simms and Thomas Russell, climbed the Cave Hill overlooking Belfast. There on the ancient McArt's Fort, they vowed famously not to 'desist in their efforts until they had subverted the authority of England and asserted Ireland's independence'.

While the authorities were suspicious of McCracken, the fact that he was a travelling cotton dealer was the perfect cover for his United Irishman activities. The work of the United Irishmen was secretive; they began a strategy of converting Catholic militia privates recruited across Ireland to their cause. However, the authorities soon undermined the United Irishmen by establishing an intelligence system to capture subversives for trial. McCracken and his fellow conspirators soon struck back at the State's intelligence apparatus, targeting both informers and their handlers. The authorities were well aware of McCracken's importance and he was eventually detained in Kilmainham Gaol in October 1796. There he endured imprisonment for thirteen months but, on release, McCracken had lost none of his revolutionary zeal and began organising in Antrim ahead of the planned rising in 1798.

McCracken was appointed to the supreme command in Antrim and led his men in an attack on the town of Antrim. Despite some initial successes, the United Irishmen were routed in a bloody encounter by a more seasoned and drilled army. With his army decimated, McCraken took refuge with a family near Slemish Mountain and sought an escape to America. On the day before he was due to travel, he was recognised and arrested. He was tried and convicted by court martial but was offered a reprieve on the condition that he give information on the other leaders. Encouraged by his own father, he refused to give the names and walked to the scaffold on the arm of his sister, Mary Ann, in Belfast's High Street on 17 July 1798. McCracken's body was originally interred in the parish church of St George, located in High Street, but his remains were later moved to Clifton Street burial ground, where he lies beside his sister. However, the actual location of his body remains a cause for dispute.

HANGED, DRAWN AND QUARTERED FOR HIGH TREASON

The suppression of the 1798 Rebellion in counties Antrim and Down did not eradicate all revolutionary passion. One of the leaders of '98, Thomas Russell, had been tried for his part in the uprising, but escaped the death penalty and was deported to mainland Europe. Celebrated in verse by Florence Mary Wilson, Russell returned to Ulster in 1803 and began making plans for a further rebellion on 23 July that year. The rebellion was an abject failure and Russell was captured and executed for his sedition on 21 October. It was said that, as far as the 1803 revolution went, Antrim was the 'sleeping dog that did not bark'.

The authorities came down heavily on those implicated in the revolutionary plot. One of the unfortunates was Andrew Hunter of Carnmoney, who appeared at the Antrim Assizes on 24 October, charged with high treason for 'making a public and cruel insurrection, rebellion and war against the King'. The list of witnesses against Hunter was long and they told of how he had showed them a letter from Russell asking them to gather in Broughshane, where 'a general would command them on an attack on Belfast'. Threatening that those who failed to join him would be hanged at their doors by the invading French, many fled the village in fear of their lives. Hunter's pleas for clemency fell on deaf ears. His trial in Carrickfergus was a fait accompli as a charge of high treason was proven. Hunter was hanged, drawn and quartered for his part in the failed uprising.

A TEMPLEPATRICK REVOLUTIONARY

In 1764, in the parish of Templepatrick, Jemmy Hope was born. His father was a weaver and Jemmy was apprenticed to the same trade. He became a journeyman weaver and worked throughout the county. He soon took an interest in politics and joined the Irish Volunteers. He felt that the fundamental question of the time was not political but social and that it could be solved only by restoring to Ireland its 'natural right of deriving their subsistence from the soil on which their labour was expended'. He was more radical than most of those who joined the United Irishmen and positively socialist in his outlook. Hope helped to organise the United Irishmen among the Presbyterian tenant farmers and farm labourers, and he led a detachment in the Battle of Antrim in 1798. He succeeded in escaping, evaded subsequent arrest and made his way to Dublin, where he was associated with Robert Emmet's plans for the 1803 uprising.

Following the failure of the 1803 revolt and the hangings of Emmet and Thomas Russell, Hope was once more a hunted man. Again, through the loyalty of friends, especially Dubliners in the Liberties, he evaded arrest. Finally, in 1806, following the death of British Prime Minister Pitt, he returned to his native Antrim, where he continued to work in the weaving trade. Hope lost his wife in 1830. He did survive her death by a further seventeen years, much of which he spent in writing. He died on 10 February 1847 and this notice of his death appeared in the *Belfast Vindicator*, 'Among men of unimpeachable character, the design of his life was the alleviation of human misery. He was full of hope to the very end.' Shortly before his death he wrote 'the soul of a nation lives on and grows strong'.

ATTACK FOILED AT TORR HEAD – 12 DECEMBER 1956

The IRA's ill-fated border campaign began at midnight on 12 December 1956. One of its first targets was a RAF radar installation on the east Antrim coast at Torr Head. Just after midnight a flying column of fifteen men, led by Cork man Tony Cooney, made its way through the darkness to a rocky outcrop off the coast road near Cushendun. For the IRA, the installation presented a relatively easy target on which to launch an attack. The reality was that the IRA squad was literally out of its depth. Composed of a scattering of ill-equipped men, the members of the unit were unsure of their terrain and were exposed in the area by their very accents.

Despite the driving rain and sleet, the column travelled by lorry to the secluded target and was on the verge of launching an attack when, by sheer chance, they happened across a patrol car containing Sergeant Bacon of the RUC in Ballymena and three members of the B-Specials. A gun battle ensued in the dead of night and the IRA squad was forced to abort the attack, abandon their lorry and flee to the surrounding hills. Three Cork men – Cooney, William Gough and Jim Linehan – were captured, as well as a Thompson sub-machine gun and a significant amount of ammunition. Only one member of the security forces, Constable Harold Thompson, was slightly injured in the skirmish when he was hit by flying glass. In the aftermath of the raid, 3,000 police and B-Specials with tracker dogs were placed on duty across north Antrim as a massive manhunt ensued for the rest of the IRA column. Despite a field-by-field search, which concentrated on the nationalist enclave of Murlough Bay, the rest of the column escaped and made their way to safety. The three Cork men arrested refused to recognise the Ballymoney court where they were charged with attempted murder and possession of ammunition the following day.

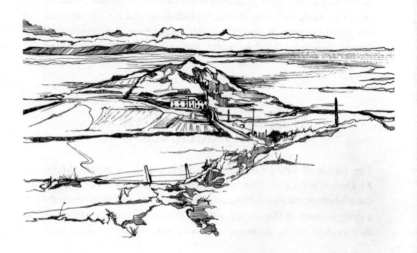

SHANE'S CASTLE IN RUINS

The Irish Troubles in the 1920s left their indelible mark on the historic Shane's Castle, near Randalstown, when the striking residence of Lord O'Neill was destroyed by the IRA during the early hours of Saturday, 20 May 1922. It is believed that up to forty men had crossed Lough Neagh from the County Tyrone side to attack the castle, while both Lord and Lady O'Neill were in residence. The violence began in the early hours when the caretaker was wakened by the barking of dogs as the assailants approached. He was seized at gunpoint and blindfolded while the castle's carpenter, John Bell, was shot in the hip during a scuffle. The gang then captured the rest of the staff and ordered the pantry boy to get petrol from an outhouse. The raiders then sprinkled large quantities of petrol over the carpets and furniture and soon the castle was ablaze. The IRA men remained within the vicinity to ensure that the building was completely alight and then fled back across Lough Neagh.

Panic spread across the countryside as the alarm was raised and the staff began in vain to fight the flames. An antiquated fire engine belonging to the Old Bleach Linen Company was commandeered and soon scores of residents from Randalstown hurried to the castle. However, it soon became apparent that it would be almost impossible to save the building. Lord O'Neill, who at 83 years of age was in very poor health, was rescued along with his wife and brought to the land steward's house. They could only look on helplessly as the building was transformed into an inferno. Whilst there was an ongoing campaign in Ireland at the time targeting stately homes, it seems that the attack was carried out specifically on Lord O'Neill as he was the father of the Right Hon. Hugh O'Neill, speaker of the newly established Northern Ireland Parliament. In December that year the Recorder's Court in Belfast awarded Lord O'Neill over £45,000 in damages for the fire.

The attack on Shane's Castle was just one attack on what seems to have been a co-ordinated night of violence across Antrim. Outside Ballymena, the historic Crebilly House, which belonged to John Black, was destroyed in a malicious fire. Amid the smouldering ruins, the charred human remains of one of the attackers were found by workmen. Police found a number of coins and a watch beside the body. It was assumed that he had been suffocated while still in the building. In addition, several houses and cars were destroyed in Larne, as was the Northern Bank in Cushendall. All telephone communications between Ballymena and Cushendall were severed and the railway line was cut. In Ballymena, the telegraph office, Eason's bookshop and the stationmaster's dwelling were destroyed.

Shane's Castle was among the most picturesque in Ireland and commanded magnificent views of Lough Neagh. Originally the stronghold had been known as Edenduff Carrick Castle, but it had been renamed in honour of Shane O'Neill, king of the O'Neill dynasty of Ulster in the mid-sixteenth century. The previous castle, which was the home of Charles Henry St John O'Neill, 1st Earl O'Neill, the then Postmaster-General of Ireland, had been burned accidentally in 1816, destroying everything except some family papers and pictures, many of historic interest. The River Maine runs through the demesne into Lough Neagh. Today all that remains of the original castle within the grounds are its ruins.

LUCKY ESCAPE FOR THE B-SPECIALS

The visit to Northern Ireland of the newly crowned King George VI and Queen Elizabeth on 28 July 1937 was marred by violence in Belfast and County Antrim. The day had commenced with the destruction of a number of customs huts along the border. As the royal couple were receiving toasts at the Belfast City Hall, a mine exploded in Academy Street, half a mile away, causing panic among the 100,000 spectators who had gathered in the city centre, many of whom were linen workers who had been afforded a full day's paid leave.

After the royal couple had left, a 16-year-old boy at Templepatrick, became alarmed when he saw three men on the railway line acting suspiciously. He immediately informed police at Templepatrick Barracks who went to the scene and discovered a biscuit tin packed with explosives. The discovery was made just before 9 p.m. Police removed the bomb shortly before a train, carrying 200 B-Specials back to Derry, passed over with its passengers oblivious to the drama. At a ceremony in November that year, the young boy who had discovered the bomb was presented with an inscribed gold watch as a mark of thanks by the Home Affairs Minister, Sir Dawson Bates.

CLYDE VALLEY FLOATING MUSEUM SCUPPERED

The *Clyde Valley*'s place in Ireland's history was cemented on 24 April 1914, when it docked in Larne Harbour with a cargo of 20,000 German rifles as part of a plan to arm the UVF during the Home Rule Crisis. During the First World War, it was acquired by the German Army and afterwards served as a fishing and coal boat in Glasgow and Nova Scotia. In 1969, the ship was acquired for £10,000 by Samuel Crawford of Whitehead and a trust was set up with the intention of turning the ship into a floating museum. On Saturday, 14 November 1969, a crowd of 5,000, led by Revd Ian Paisley, turned up at Larne Harbour to see the return of ship.

The Unionist government at Stormont boycotted the event in protest at what they saw as Paisley's attempt to gain political capital, but the 'Big Man' was cheered enthusiastically as he addressed the freezing crowds. The *Clyde Valley* then travelled to Carrickfergus, where, with no funding secured to transform it into a 'floating museum to the principles of loyalist Protestantism', it lay rusting. In 1975, having accrued significant berthing debts and posing an obstruction to other yachts and small craft, it was bought by a scrap-metal company from Bury and towed across the Irish Sea. There it was moored in the River Lune until finally it was broken up for scrap.

ANTRIM'S PRESIDENTIAL LINKS

Grover Cleveland was President of the United States on two occasions (1885 to 1889 and 1893 to 1897) and was of County Antrim descent on his mother's side. In the 1790s, his maternal grandfather Abner Neal emigrated from County Antrim to Baltimore, where he established a printworks.

Andrew Jackson, who served as President of the United States from 1829 to 1837, was the son of County Antrim parents. Andrew Senior and Elizabeth Jackson hailed originally from the small village of Boneybefore, which lies a mile to the north of Carrickfergus. They sailed for America in 1765 and their original homestead in Antrim was pulled down to make way for the Belfast-to-Larne railway in the 1860s. The site of the Jackson cottage is now the location of the Andrew Jackson Centre, which is a replica of the home rebuilt in the style of the former building. In 2016, it was announced that the United States Mint would move the face of Jackson from the front to the back of the $20 note and that of the female anti-slavery campaigner Harriet Tubman would appear on the front of the note. Jackson owned hundreds of slaves who worked on his Hermitage Plantation in Tennessee. He was, however, a complex character and he and his wife Rachael famously adopted two Native American children.

Richard Milhous Nixon, President of the United States from 1972 until he was impeached in 1974, was descended from James Moore, who was born in Ballymoney in 1777. Another ancestor, Thomas Milhous, was born in Carrickfergus in 1699.

PRESIDENTIAL HOMESTEAD
SAVED FROM DESTRUCTION

William McKinley (1843–1901) became the twenty-fifth President of the United States in 1897 and served until his assassination on 14 September 1901 at the hands of the Italian anarchist Leon Czolgosz. Born in Ohio, McKinley's great-grandfather, James, emigrated from Ireland to the United States in 1743 from the small homestead of Conagher, which is situated between Ballymoney and Dervock. The McKinley homestead remained in the family's hands and, in 1798, a Francis McKinley was executed in Coleraine for his part in the United Irishmen's uprising. The farm was inherited by his sons, John and Francis. However, the last member of the McKinley clan left for the United States in 1839. The McKinleys' ancestral home was due for demolition until it was rescued and rebuilt in the Ulster American Folk Park in Omagh in 1996.

BRUTAL ASSASSINATION IN LISBURN

Sectarian violence engulfed the town of Lisburn in the aftermath of the assassination of RIC District Inspector Oswald Swanzy on Sunday, 22 August 1920. Swanzy had been in charge of police operations in north Cork City at the time of the murder of Tomás MacCurtain, the Sinn Féin Lord Mayor of Cork, in March that year and was widely believed by nationalists to have been involved in the killing. Swanzy, a native of County Monaghan, had been transferred to Lisburn shortly after the murder of MacCurtain. However, a decision to target Swanzy was taken personally by Michael Collins, who acted on a tip-off from RIC Sergeant Matt McCarthy, who provided information that the detective inspector was based in the County Antrim town. Collins sent IRA intelligence officer Sean Culhane to Belfast to organise the assassination and he, along with Belfast IRA men, set up an ambush outside Lisburn Cathedral.

As Swanzy left church he was shot at close range by Culhane and Belfast IRA man Roger McCorley. The IRA gang escaped by taxi, but the news of the outrage set off a carnival of sectarian violence against the Catholic residents of the town. Mobs went on the rampage and burned the Hibernian Hall in Smithfield and attacked other Catholic-owned houses and businesses. The violence against the Catholic population lasted for three days and over 1,000 fled to Belfast and had to endure attacks from mobs which had gathered at Hilden and Lambeg. At Sunday Mass in Lisburn on 29 August, a total of nine people were present, such was the fear of further attacks. Swanzy was buried at Mount Jerome Cemetery in Dublin on 25 August and is commemorated with a plaque in Lisburn Cathedral, which reads:

> In proud and loving memory of Oswald Ross Swanzy, DI
> Royal Irish Constabulary, who gave his life in Lisburn on
> Sunday August 22, 1920 and his gallant comrades who, like

him, have been killed in the unfaltering discharge of their
duty and in the service of their country. Be thou faithful unto
death and I will give you a crown of life.

BALLYCASTLE BANK RAID

The boycotting of Catholic businesses in Belfast at the height of
the 1922 Troubles impacted on Ballycastle when the local Ulster
Bank was robbed on 29 March 1922. Three armed and masked
men stormed the bank during the lunch hour and demanded money
for the 'Catholics of Belfast'. The manager, Mr J.B.R. Harper, and
his assistant Mr McCabe were locked in a lavatory while the raiders
set about opening the safe. They escaped with over £7,000 and fled
into the surrounding countryside. The manager, using a penknife,
eventually unlocked the door and raised the alarm.

LORD CUSHENDUN AND WINSTON CHURCHILL

Winston Churchill had extensive links with County Antrim, but it
was his father, Lord Randolph Churchill, who has been indelibly
linked with the cause of Ulster Unionism. During the Home Rule
Crisis of 1886, he uttered the famous phrase 'Ulster will fight
and Ulster will be right'. In that speech, which was delivered at
Ulster Hall on 22 February that year, Randolph, perhaps, set in
motion the events that led to the partitioning of Ireland in 1921.
Arriving in Larne, Churchill travelled to Belfast and gave a rousing
speech which argued that there were 'not one but two Irelands and
[that] and it would be unjust to hand over Irish loyalists [Unionists]
to the mercy of a native government'.

By 1912, the Home Rule debate remained unresolved. However,
Randolph's son and Liberal MP, Winston Churchill, then First
Lord of the Admiralty, had become a supporter of Home Rule and
travelled to Belfast to speak in favour of the nationalist cause at,
ironically, the Ulster Hall. The indignation felt by Unionists was such
that a mass blockade of the hall was organised and Churchill was
forced to make his speech at Celtic Park, which was located close

to the nationalist Falls Road. Churchill did not win many Unionist friends in Belfast, referring to the Carsonite movement as 'an extra-Parliamentary force which Britain's Tory Party was using to destroy the power of Parliament'.

To Unionists, Churchill was a traitor and in the House of Commons in November that year he was to feel the physical manifestations of that anger. During a debate, Churchill had taunted the Conservative and Unionist members by waving his handkerchief at them. After one particular biting remark, Ronald McNeill MP, a prominent Orangeman and son of a wealthy Antrim landowner, lost his temper and hurled a bound copy of the standing orders in Churchill's direction. McNeill's aim was true and Churchill's face, it was reported, was severely bruised by the book, which left him with three visible cuts and considerable swelling. Both men then made to square up on the floor as members crowded about awaiting fisticuffs. However, order was restored when the Labour MP Will Crooks struck up the first line of 'Auld Lang Syne', which added a dash of comedy to the nascent battle and defused the situation. With hindsight, perhaps Churchill thought twice about taking on McNeill, since the latter, at 6ft 6in, was considered to be the tallest MP to have graced the Commons. Irish Parliamentary Party MP John Dillon described the scene by saying, 'The language used was so disgraceful that any chance crowd collected from the lowest slums of London could not improve upon it. The scene was more like an explosion of drunken rowdyism than the proceedings of an elected assembly.'

Ronald John McNeill (1861–1934) was born in Torquay to a Scots-Irish family which hailed from Cushendun. He was educated at Harrow and Oxford and took up a career in journalism before entering parliament in 1911 as the Conservative and Unionist MP for Canterbury. Throughout the Home Rule period, McNeill was one of the most prominent and vociferous figures on the Unionist side. He was a stormy personality who was said to have favoured 'abuse rather than logical argument', but was elevated to the House of Lords in November 1927, when he took the name Lord Cushendun. The family's spectacular homestead, called 'Craigdun', is located near Cullybackey, where McNeill died on 12 October 1934.

PRESIDENT KENNEDY AND
THE GIANT'S CAUSEWAY

One of Captain Terence O'Neill's first acts as Prime Minister of Northern Ireland threw the Unionist hierarchy into disarray. O'Neill assumed office in late March 1963, when rumours of a visit to the Republic of Ireland by US President John F. Kennedy were rife. In an attempt to create new political ground, O'Neill, with the backing of Prime Minister Harold MacMillan, extended a personal invitation to Kennedy to open the new Giant's Causeway Park in May that year. However, the date for the President's visit to the south was confirmed for late June 1963 and a polite letter of regret was received at Stormont Castle. Despite this, rumours abounded that pressure to refuse the invitation had been exerted on Kennedy from within the Democratic Party, many of whose members were sympathetic to Irish nationalism. O'Neill was ridiculed by Nationalist MPs within the Stormont parliament for Kennedy's 'polite refusal' and it was suggested that the President of Ireland, Éamon de Valera, should be invited to perform the honours on 16 May. That suggestion, not surprisingly, was rejected and it fell to O'Neill to cut the tape at the ceremony. During his visit to the Republic, Kennedy was presented with a piece of the causeway by Andrew Minihan, chair of the Antrim urban council, at New Ross, County Wexford. The piece of rock was delivered by helicopter and had been inscribed, 'To John Fitzgerald Kennedy – From the People of North Antrim'. Ironically, it is thought that John F. Kennedy had visited the Giant's Causeway with his father in the late 1930s, when Joseph Kennedy Sr had been ambassador to the United Kingdom.

COUNTY ANTRIM-BORN
PREMIER OF NEW ZEALAND

Born in Glenavy, County Antrim, in 1839, John Ballance became New Zealand's fourteenth premier in 1891 and held office until his death in 1893. His father, Samuel Ballance, had been a tenant farmer on the Marquis of Hertford's estate, near Lisburn, while his mother, Mary McNeice, was a member of the local Quaker community. John Ballance was apprenticed to an ironmonger in Belfast at the age of 14 and emigrated from Ireland to New Zealand in 1866, at the age of 27. There he established the *Wanganui Herald* newspaper and became interested in politics, founding the New Zealand Liberal Party. In 1868, during the Maori War, he joined the local cavalry but was dismissed after his criticism of the military campaign was published in his newspaper. He was elected to the House of Representatives in 1875 and enjoyed a rapid rise through government, becoming leader of the Liberal opposition during the term of office of Harry Atkinson. He assumed office after the 1890 election, during which time the county grew economically and he was known as a strong advocate of women's suffrage. He died of heart disease in April 1893 and is commemorated by a statue outside the Parliamentary Library in Wellington. The restored home of the Ballance family is now a tourist attraction which is operated by the Ulster New Zealand Trust and is situated on the Lisburn Road outside Glenavy.

ELECTORAL SHENANIGANS IN SOUTH ANTRIM

The 1903 Westminster by-election for South Antrim brought two strains of Unionism into direct opposition. It was held after the sitting Unionist MP, William Ellison-Macartney, had left the Commons to take up the post of Deputy-Master of the Royal Mint. Doctor Samuel Keightley was a significant figure in public life as a prominent 'Liberal' Unionist who was pitted against the Conservative and Unionist candidate Charles Craig, the brother of the future Prime Minister of Northern Ireland, James Craig. Keightley was a 'Russellite', a political party named after Thomas Russell, Liberal Unionist for South Tyrone, a group which advocated progressive land reform and the transfer of land from land owners to tenant farmers. However, there was to be a bitter battle in the hinterland of South Antrim as one householder was to find to his cost.

On Saturday, 7 February, a shopkeeper in Antrim town, who also acted as the election agent to Dr Keightley, awoke to the rancid smell of tar permeating his house. On opening his door he discovered that the front of his house, doors and windows had been completely covered with a thick coating of the substance. Such was the extent of the damage that police officers believed the culprits had been at their work for at least six hours. At the election the following Tuesday, Craig was declared the victor with 4,564, while Doctor Keightley trailed behind with 3,615.

BRIBERY AND CORRUPTION IN LISBURN

The election of local mill-owner John Dougherty Barbour to the House of Commons for the town of Lisburn in February 1863 was controversial in many ways. At the time, Lisburn was considered to be staunchly 'true blue' Tory, but when the 'Liberal radical' Barbour was victorious over the Tory Edwin Verner by six votes, many eyebrows were raised and soon talk of corruption spread through the town. Presently, rumours began circulating that twenty electors had been wined and dined over nine days at Barbour's home at Hilden House. It was soon discovered that, during what was described as an 'orgy', bribes were given to some present at Barbour's house to secure his election.

Matters took a turn for the worse on 30 March, when an Orange parade marched through Lisburn to Barbour's house to protest the result. The march became violent as it passed the Catholic chapel and soon pistol shots rang out amid the trouble. On reaching Hilden House, the angry marchers dispersed when they discovered that the MP was still in London. However, more violence erupted in the town on the parade's return as anger over the result manifested itself on the streets. In June that year, the result of the election was deemed void as a parliamentary commission found that Barbour had been guilty of corrupt practices, having secured a number of votes through 'coercion and bribery'. In the ensuing by-election, Verner took the seat, beating Barbour by 151 votes to 90.

SIR ROGER CASEMENT

Roger David Casement (1864–1916) was born in Sandymount, County Dublin, to a Protestant father and a Catholic mother. His family hailed originally from County Antrim, but Casement spent his early days in Dublin, where his mother, Anne Jephson, died in 1873, and his father, Roger Senior, died in 1877. Casement was then sent to live with his uncle, John Casement, in Magherintemple near Ballycastle and was educated at the Ballymena Academy. He joined the diplomatic service and received a knighthood in 1911 for his investigative work into human rights abuses in Peru. Such charitable work turned Casement into a dedicated anti-colonialist and he retired from his work as a diplomat to dedicate himself to the cause of Irish nationalism.

He was convinced that any successful rebellion in Ireland would need assistance from Germany and travelled to the Continent during the First World War to raise a battalion of Irish prisoners-of-war. In an attempt to delay the Easter Rising, he travelled to Ireland in a German U-boat and, although he landed safely at Banna Strand in Kerry, he was arrested the following day and transported to the Tower of London. After a three-day trial, he was found guilty of high treason and executed on 3 August 1916. His dying wish, spoken from the dock, was, 'When they have done with me, don't let my bones rest in this dreadful place. Take me back to Ireland and let me lie there.' This wish was granted in 1965, when his remains were transported home and he was afforded a State funeral in Dublin.

REMEMBRANCE DAY ROW IN BALLYMENA

In 1977, an invitation by the Royal British Legion to a Catholic priest to officiate at the annual Remembrance Day service in Ballymena incurred the wrath of the local DUP councillors. The selection of Fr Hugh Murphy from Ahoghill, a former RAF chaplain who had been decorated for his service during the war, led to a boycott of the service by the DUP councillors, who opted to hold an alternative service.

4

CRIME AND PUNISHMENT

ANTRIM'S ALCATRAZ
PLANNED FOR RATHLIN

With the onslaught of the Troubles in 1969, the Stormont government considered plans to create an Alcatraz-style prison on Rathlin Island. The antiquated prison on Belfast's Crumlin Road was not considered escape-proof and so there was speculation that a new facility would be built on the island. The rumour became prevalent in Stormont on 11 January 1972, following a disclosure by Prime Minister Brian Faulkner that detailed consideration was being given to Sir Charles Cunningham's report and his recommendation that a secure prison of modern design be constructed. In early 1971, British paratroopers had landed on the Rathlin, but their presence remained a mystery to the islanders. With the introduction of internment in August that year, a theory circulated that the troops had been sent to Rathlin to assess the island's suitability as a location for an internment camp.

The publication of the Cunningham Report made it clear the existing prisons in Northern Ireland were not fit for purpose. Cunningham ruled out the Copeland Islands, off the coast of north Down, but it was suggested by Captain Robert Mitchell MP that Rathlin would be suitable if the residents were evacuated from it. The islanders reacted swiftly to this suggestion. Tony McCuaig, owner of the only pub on the island, was incensed, stating that Captain Mitchell 'would never see the people of this island evacuated'. He emphasised that his was a statement of the spirit of the people and not of intent. He added that the people on the island did not bother much about politics but, if they did, they would be Republican.

DEPORTED FOR LIFE FOR COW STEALING

The *Belfast News Letter* reported, on 26 September 1833, the passing through the town of a band of convicts on their way from Carrickfergus to Kingstown (now Dún Laoghaire), where they were to be deported to New South Wales. The men, it was noted, were 'clean and well dressed and seemed to be in good spirits' as they passed through Belfast by cart and caravan, accompanied by a guard of soldiers. It was reported that, on leaving Carrickfergus, the men 'uttered not a word of complaint, but expressions of thanks' to the keeper of the jail, Mr Samuel Erskine. The men were transported for the following offences: Hugh McLaughlin (58), Samuel Lorimer (35), Andrew Blair (83), James Hempbill (40) Samuel Falloon (29) and Samuel Johnston (38) were all transported for life for stealing cattle while James Mackay (19), Edward Burke, John Savage (36), John Graham (20) and Armstrong Edmonston (40) were transported for seven years for theft.

'GOD TOLD ME TO DO IT!'

The lodging house kept by 80-year-old widow Sarah McHurley was the scene of a brutal murder on the night of 30 November 1897, when a lodger, John Hurley (no relation), murdered the proprietor as she lay in her bed. Hurley, who came from Broughshane, was staying in the house and was said to have become 'suddenly demented' at midnight, entering the widow's bedroom and murdering her with a kitchen knife. The screams of the old woman alerted the other lodgers, who ran to the room where they too were attacked by Hurley. Eventually, Hurley was subdued and when the police arrived he said, 'God told me to do it!' When brought before the magistrate, Hurley, who was described as a 'wandering tramp', was 'quite unconcerned' by the incident. The newspapers reported the murder in all its gory under the headline, 'Mad Tramp's Desperate Deed'.

RIBBONMEN INDICTED IN BRUTAL ATTACK

The Ribbon Society, a largely Catholic sect which sought to prevent landlords from charging exorbitant rents or evicting poor tenants from their land, was strong throughout Ireland in the early part of the nineteenth century.

It was believed that on 12 May 1828 Ribbonmen attacked and killed Alexander Brownlee, 'a respectable character, unconnected to any political party', as he travelled home to Kells, 5 miles from Antrim town. However, once the case came to court it was revealed that Brownlee had been attacked in what was a drunken sectarian attack.

Brownlee was travelling home that evening from Antrim fair with a father and son, John and Robert Cooper, when they were attacked by upwards of twelve men who had secreted themselves in a ditch near Dunsilly. The men and boy were subjected to a 'barbaric and inhuman' attack with stones and sticks and left for dead on the highway. Brownlee survived until the following morning but succumbed due to a fractured skull. The Coopers were badly injured. With a reward of £500 offered for information that would lead to the capture of the attackers, seven men were soon charged with the murder and tried at Carrickfergus.

It seems that Brownlee had been attacked in Antrim earlier that day by a drunken mob who had accused him of leading an Orange band through the town at Easter. When the attack was broken up by police, the mob set up an ambush at Dunsilly, where the murder took place. One of the attackers, James Moran, was alleged to have run after Brownlee shouting, 'To Hell with your soul, what can King Billy do for you now?' The seven men were, however, not thought to have been the ringleaders and were acquitted of murder, with four being convicted of rioting and sentenced to eighteen months' hard labour.

THE MORALLY BANKRUPT SCHOOLMASTER

A strange case was heard at the Dublin debtors' court in March 1832, when Robert Fryars sued George Reid for £4 12s, that being the amount Fryars believed he was owed for the alleged seduction of his daughter by Reid. The case was taken against Reid, a schoolteacher from Soldierstown, near Aghalee, after Fryars' daughter had fallen pregnant to the teacher. Reid's attorney, Mr MacNally, while admitting that the teacher had 'loose morals', pointed out that his client was bankrupt and could not pay maintenance on account of his poverty. MacNally suggested that Reid had 'like other young men, been addicted to fashionable follies', adding that a very short custodial sentence would, perhaps, be appropriate since it could act as a deterrent to other schoolteachers. Such a sentence, said MacNally, 'would teach them [schoolmasters] that their duty was to inculcate morality and not to circulate vice'. Reid, 'who exhibited anything but a seductive appearance in the dock', was warned that he should seek to compensate his creditor or face the fullest sentence of the court. Reid, wisely, made provision to settle the debt, but was never to return to Soldierstown or indeed the teaching profession.

WORKHOUSE MOTHER SELLS HER CHILD

An extraordinary case of a mother selling her child was before the Belfast board of guardians last week. The subject was introduced by the reading of an entry in the Catholic chaplain's book, drawing attention to the fact that on Friday week a lady and a gentleman by promises induced an inmate named Ellen McKenna to sell her infant child, four months old. The mother having consented, the child was taken away, it is supposed, to Leeds, as the parties gave that address. The mother afterwards repented of her unnatural act, and wished to have the child restored. After a long discussion, the board were of the opinion that none of the officers were to blame in connection with the proceeding, and refused to take any action in restoring the child to the mother.

(*The Nation*, 13 November 1875)

THE PHILOSOPHICAL CONVICT

At Antrim Assizes on 5 May 1821 a man by the name of Stewart was convicted of stealing a hat and sentenced to be transported to Botany Bay for seven years. On receiving the sentence, the *Freeman's Journal* reported that Stewart remained philosophical, telling the judge, 'Well, at least it's better than a bad marriage.'

BAND OF ROBBERS CAPTURED

Between 1815 and 1817, houses in the rural townlands between Ballyclare and Antrim had been subjected to a series of vicious robberies by a band of robbers. Their crime spree came to an abrupt end on 2 January 1817, when the criminals tried to ransack the home of a yeoman, Robert Miller, who lived near Donegore, between the two towns. News had spread that a number of homes had been ransacked in Antrim that evening and Miller sat in the darkness in his home, fearing an attack. In the middle of the night, the robbers arrived and demanded that Miller hand over his musket. After breaking windows in the property, Miller discharged his musket at the robbers, injuring one of them, David Warwick, and causing the rest of the group to scatter. Undeterred, Miller and a neighbour set off in pursuit and took the injured Warwick back to Milller's house, where he was told that 'he would have his brains blown out' if he did not give Miller the names of the others involved. With his dying breath, Warwick, a man of undoubted principle and loyalty to his comrades, told Miller the names and addresses of all his accomplices, who were then captured and imprisoned.

THE JUDGE AND THE COBBLESTONE

The strange case of Robert Gordon came before the Ulster Assizes in December 1898, when the prisoner was charged with attempting to break into – not out of! – Antrim Workhouse. Described as 'a rough-looking man', Gordon was sentenced to twelve months' hard labour by Sir Peter O'Brien, Lord Chief Justice of Ireland. Immediately, Gordon uttered a tirade of abuse, sprang to the edge of the dock and threw a large cobblestone at head of the judge. The missile crashed against the panelling behind Sir Peter, missing him by inches. A violent scene ensued as warders and police grappled with the prisoner, who was eventually taken down and, no doubt, administered physical chastisement. The bemused and shaken judge picked up and examined the stone which lay at his feet and handed it over to a somewhat embarrassed clerk.

MOTHER AND SON HANGED FOR POISONING

The death by hanging of Esther Loughbridge, 'a woman of about 78 years', together with her blind son, Hugh, at Carrickfergus on Monday, 16 August 1824, took place on the 'new drop' at the town's jail. The two had been found guilty of poisoning Hugh's wife, Hannah (*née* Houston), at the family's home at Coole, near Carnmoney.

During the trial a witness, John Irwin, told the jury how he had accompanied Hugh Longbridge to Mr Price's shop at Knockagh, where the defendant had bought three pennies' worth of rat poison to deal with vermin 'who were destroying his butter'. Later that day, Hannah fell ill after eating some bread and potatoes and neighbours were called to tend to the woman. Complaining that 'her heart was on fire', she died two days later and was buried without an inquest. On exhuming the body traces of arsenic were discovered and the mother and son were arrested, tried and sentenced to death. Standing awaiting his fate on the gallows, Hugh sang Psalm 23 and other prisoners joined in. His mother, when the rope was placed around her neck, exclaimed, 'Eh, dear me. That's surely the hardest thing that's ever been tied.' The old lady's assertion that the rope had been too tight was in vain as the execution proceeded regardless. The two fell to their death simultaneously and their bodies were transported to Lisburn Infirmary for dissection.

NAKED BODY IN A FIELD – AMERICAN HANGED

The discovery of the body of Achmet Musa on 4 September 1931 in a field at Seskin, near Carrickfergus, set off a manhunt which ended in the arrest of Eddie Cullens, a 27-year-old American citizen. Both men were members of a circus group that had travelled to Belfast from Liverpool and stayed in Ryan's Hotel on Donegall Quay, leaving on 2 September. While in Belfast, the men had driven to Bangor, County Down, accompanied by two local women, one of whom noticed a blue-and-white bathing cap in the glove compartment of the car. The bathing cap would become a vital piece of evidence in the case.

Musa's bloodied body was discovered naked, except for the bathing cap, by a man riding a horse close to Seskin. He had grown suspicious when the horse had become alarmed and refused to pass a hedge beside the field. Later that day in Belfast, a bag of bloodied clothes was discovered in a doorway in Church Lane in Belfast and police began searching for Cullens. By this stage Cullens had fled to England, but he was captured in London and police seized his revolver, which matched the weapon that had administered the fatal shot. Cullens was taken back to Belfast and was found guilty of the murder, primarily due to the evidence of the girl who had seen the bathing cap, and sentenced to hang. A plea for a pardon on the grounds of his American citizenship was refused. Cullens walked to the scaffold in Crumlin Road Prison accompanied by the Belfast rabbi, Jacob Schater, on the morning of 13 January 1932. He was the thirteenth man to have been hanged at the prison.

CRUEL MURDER OF A GRANDCHILD

In April 1830, Jane Graham was charged with the murder of her grandchild, William John Bashford Bell, by administering poison at the Farmer's Glen, near Magheragall. The child's mother Eliza

Graham had given birth 'out of wedlock' and employed a nurse, Mary Hamilton, to care for the infant. Jane Graham was a frequent visitor to the house and she came on 9 August to visit her daughter. While she was there, the child began to cry uncontrollably. Graham instructed the nurse to 'beat it, for that it had not the cry of a child, but of a young devil'. The child was soothed and placed in its cradle. Graham told the nurse to go to a neighbour, Betty Gorman, to get some broth. On her return, the child was awake but unwell. After ten minutes the infant began to vomit a white substance and a doctor was called, but the child was dead when he arrived.

Suspicions were aroused and Jane Graham was arrested when the autopsy discovered that the infant had been poisoned. At the subsequent case at Carrickfergus, a young neighbour, John Doran, testified that he had seen Graham put something 'white like flour' into the child's mouth with her finger and thumb while it was in the cradle. Dr William Thomson of Lisburn reported that the post-mortem examination of the deceased had revealed that the stomach was very much inflamed by a considerable quantity of arsenic. Graham gave no evidence in defence and the jury returned a verdict of guilty. The judge put on the fatal black cap and, after a most impressive and admonishment address to the prisoner, sentenced her to be executed on Wednesday and her body thereafter to be given for dissection. She was hanged at a public ceremony on 31 March. The *Belfast News Letter* described her as 'a wretched woman who expiated her crime by the forfeiture of her own life, at the usual place of execution, at Carrickfergus'.

A PEACEFUL YEAR IN COUNTY ANTRIM

Despite the world standing on the cusp of the Great War in 1914, an unusual ceremony took place at the County Antrim Quarter Session at the Crumlin Road Courthouse in January that year. As His Honour Judge Craig awaited the start of proceedings, it was announced in the court that there 'was no criminal business to be dealt with'. As was the ancient custom in such circumstances, it fell to the county sub-sheriff, Mr Bristow, to present the judge with a pair of white gloves as a symbol 'of the peaceful state of the county'. It was, in fact, the second occasion within the sub-sheriff's year-long reign that there had been no criminal proceedings to bring before the judge. The Clerk of the Crown and Peace, Mr H. McNeill-McCormick, indicated that in his long experience such an occurrence was unprecedented. He added that he 'sincerely wished for the continuance in the county of the happy state of affairs which existed at present'.

SHOCKING DOUBLE MURDER IN ARMOY – TWO SISTERS SHOT DEAD

On the afternoon of 24 May 1928, a shocking double murder took place at Mullaghduff, about a mile from the village of Armoy, the victims being Miss Maggie Macauley (43) and her sister, Miss Sarah Macauley (38). The discovery of the dead bodies was made by a servant, Kate Murdoch, who told the inquest that she found the two sisters lying in the kitchen beside the family shotgun with their heads and faces mutilated. When the sisters' brothers arrived at the house, they found that £30 was missing from a cashbox and a gold watch and chain were also missing from a vest pocket.

After the inquest, a farmworker, William Smylie, who had given evidence, was arrested and his house was searched by the RUC. The missing money was found in a boot and he was charged with the crime at Ballycastle on 1 June. Smylie admitted to police that he had stolen the money, but claimed that he had not murdered the sisters. On appearing in court, Smylie often glanced towards his wife, who had their young baby in her arms. Several times the baby cried out pathetically 'Dada' for his father and was eventually removed from court. On Tuesday 10 July, Smylie was found guilty only of the murder of Sarah Macauley and sentenced to be hanged at Crumlin Road Jail on 8 August. The judge told Smylie, 'You gave those two unfortunate women not a moment before you hurled them into eternity'. A final plea for clemency was dismissed and Smylie, an ex-soldier who had served in the Great War, admitted his guilt in writing before the sentence was carried out. He was hanged in Belfast by the executioner Thomas Pierrepoint.

WITCHCRAFT TRIALS IN CARRICKFERGUS

In March 1711, eight women from the east Antrim area appeared in court in Carrickfergus and were found guilty of witchcraft, earning each of them a year's imprisonment for the 'demonic possession of the body, mind and spirit of a teenage girl', Mary Dunbar. Despite the removal from the Irish statute books of the crime of witchcraft in 1586, the trial caused a total sensation in Ireland and beyond. With the Plantation of Ulster in the 1700s, many of the Scottish Presbyterian settlers brought with them strong beliefs in witchcraft. At that time, Islandmagee was home to about 3,000 people, most of them settlers with strong religious convictions, as well as a deep belief in sorcery and superstition.

The incident at Islandmagee began in September 1710, when a widow, Mrs Anne Haltridge, began to experience supernatural phenomena at her home, Knowehead House. Situated on the Islandmagee peninsula, Mrs Haltridge's house was attacked by an unseen hand with stones and turf and she woke many mornings to find that her bedclothes and pillows had been violently removed. Soon a 'ragged boy' began visiting her house and locals became concerned when stories of his ability to disappear into thin air spread. By this stage, Mrs Haltrige had become ill and died, in February 1711, just after a teenage cousin, Mary Dunbar, moved into the house to help out with chores.

Dunbar's presence only added to suspicions in the area of a demonic presence in the house. Within hours of her arrival, Mary said that she had found a five-knotted apron lying on the parlour floor, triggering a series of supernatural disturbances (this it was felt was proof of the existence of a witch in the house). Soon, local women claimed that the girl had exhibited signs of possession: issuing vile threats, blaspheming and experiencing violent fits when clergymen visited. Dunbar went to the authorities and claimed that eight women from the vicinity had tortured her and kept her captive in the house, force-feeding her with feathers, pins and buttons. The Mayor of Carrickfergus, Edward Clements, led a witch-hunt, had the eight women arrested and charged them with 'bewitching' Dunbar. The women were Janet Latimer of Irish Quarter, Carrickfergus; Janet Millar of Scotch Quarter, Carrickfergus; Janet Main of Broad Island; and Margaret Mitchell of Kilroot; together with Catherine McCalmond, Janet Liston, Elizabeth Sellor and Janet Carson, all from Islandmagee.

The trial, held in late March in front of Judge Anthony Upton, was a sensation. Many of the nineteen witnesses, which included four clergymen, spoke of the accused women's sobriety and their regular attendance at church and tried to blacken the name of Mary Dunbar. Dunbar was unable to testify at the trial as she claimed to be terrified and to have been struck dumb. The jury, however, found the women guilty of witchcraft and they each received twelve-month sentences. During their captivity they were bound in chains and exhibited publicly at the town's stocks on four occasions. It is said that one of the women lost an eye, such was the viciousness if the attacks that they were subjected to. All records of Mary Dunbar vanished after the trial.

The story took an ironic twist in early 2015, when a request was made to Larne Borough Council to erect a plaque commemorating the convicted women at the new Gobbins Visitor Centre. The proposal had been submitted by Martina Devlin, a local journalist, who wished to highlight the plight the women had endured. Not everyone on the council was supportive though and a local Unionist councillor, Jack McKee, opposed the idea, describing it as 'anti-God'. He added that he could not support the proposal, saying that the plaque would become a 'shrine to paganism'. He added that he 'could not tell whether or not the women had been rightly or wrongly convicted as he didn't have the facts, but was not going to support devil worship'.

THE MURDER AND A COVER-UP IN 'THE GLEN' – 1952

The murder of Patricia Curran in Whiteabbey in November 1952 was a sensation that placed Antrim town in the world spotlight. The 19-year-old daughter of Judge Lancelot Curran and Lady Doris Curran was found dead in the grounds of the extensive family property, The Glen, sparking a murder hunt that led to the conviction of an innocent man, Iain Hay Gordon. Patricia was a student at Belfast's Queen's University and was known to be a free spirit. She smoked, drank, dated married men and had recently taken up a job as a delivery-van driver. Her body, which had been stabbed thirty-seven times, was discovered late on the evening of 12 November by her father, her brother and the family's solicitor beside the driveway on the grounds. Despite the fact that it had been raining, Patricia's body was dry, as were her belongings, which were found close by. The trio, in a departure from standard practice, moved the body to a nearby doctor's house, telling a policeman she was still alive, despite one arm being stiff with rigor mortis.

Soon a massive murder hunt was launched under the famous John Capstick of Scotland Yard. Interestingly, Judge Curran did not let police into his home until almost a week after the murder, during which time Patricia's bedroom had been redecorated. This fuelled rumours that Patricia had been killed at The Glen during a domestic dispute, with Doris Curran coming under scrutiny. Police then began to concentrate their enquiries on a young, impressionable Scots-born RAF technician called Iain Hay Gordon, a friend of Desmond who had visited the Curran home and had become infatuated by Patricia. The RUC conducted 40,000 interviews in relation to the case, but, in what was seen as an act of desperation, Gordon was arrested, despite the fact that there was no significant evidence against him. He confessed and in March 1953 he was found 'guilty but insane'. He was sentenced to be detained at Antrim's Holywell Hospital. Later he was to claim that he had signed his confession only because detectives threatened to tell his parents that he was homosexual. He served seven years in the mental hospital before being released by the then Unionist Home Affairs Minister Brian Faulkner in 1960 on the condition that he change his name and not talk publicly about the case.

Gordon, or 'John Cameron' as he was known, refused to accept his conviction and was eventually cleared of the murder in 2000 by the Court of Appeal in Belfast. It was a verdict that marked the end of one of the longest enduring miscarriages of justice in the British Isles. The court had heard an abundance of new evidence, which exposed the flawed case that the prosecution had presented in 1953. With the case again coming under severe public scrutiny, many people believe that the family had been attempting to protect Doris Curran.

In 1957, Desmond Curran, Patricia's brother, renounced his Presbyterian faith, began training for the priesthood and was ordained in Rome in 1964. The ceremony was attended by Judge Curran, a senior Orangeman and member of the Unionist establishment, while Doris Curran was unable attend as she was detained in a Belfast clinic. He worked for many years in South Africa and many felt that this was his escape from the burden he had been weighed down with by after his sister's death. He died in 2015.

Patricia, Lancelot and Doris Curran are buried in the family's grave at Drumbeg 5 miles outside Belfast.

With the death of Desmond, the truth of what happened to Patricia Curran may be lost forever. However, the events of that night in The Glen remain a cause for public conjecture. At the time of the murder, RUC County Inspector Albert Kennedy, who initially headed the inquiry, wrote, 'It was decided to pursue every other line of inquiry before allowing our thoughts to concentrate on something which seemed too fantastic to believe, namely, that the Currans were in fact covering up the murderer and telling a tissue of lies.' It is a case that will not go away.

WHIPPED AND FLOGGED FOR RIOTING

On 2 March 1815, a meeting of local landholders in Antrim town ended in a serious riot after a handbill calling for a protest had been circulated among the 'lower orders'. The bill had asked people to 'save your families from starvation and famine' by gathering in the town on market day, when the meeting had been scheduled. With the landholders' meeting in a local inn, the drunken mob ('chiefly women, abetted by men') attacked the public house, forcing the gentry to flee to the local courthouse. The constabulary soon arrived in force and arrested the ringleaders, who were tried at Carrickfergus the following week.

Two of those arrested, Arthur Skeffington and William Jackson, were sentenced to be imprisoned and to be publicly whipped in Belfast on 2 April. With the aim of setting an example for others, the men were paraded outside the Exchange in Belfast that morning and then stripped and tied to the back of a cart. As they processed through the main streets of the town, the executioner flogged the two men and soon an angry crowd gathered. A riot ensued as a cart carrying bricks was taken by the mob and the sub-sheriff of Antrim, Joseph Fulton, was knocked unconscious, losing two teeth in the process. The police were called and rescued the official party, and the cart made its way back to Carrickfergus, where the men began ten-year sentences.

5

A SPORTING COUNTY

WILLIE JOHN MCBRIDE –
WORLD RUGBY LEGEND

Born in Toomebridge in 1940, Willie John McBride represented
Ireland with distinction on the rugby field on sixty-three occasions,
eleven times as captain. He also appeared seventeen times for the
British Lions and in 1997 was inducted into the International
Rugby Hall of Fame. His love of rugby was harnessed at Ballymena
Academy and he went on to represent that town's rugby club.
In 1961 he made his debut for Ulster and a year later he was
chosen for Ireland against England at Twickenham. His career in
the green jersey saw Ireland enjoy notable victories over South
Africa and Australia. His final match for Ireland was against Wales
in Cardiff in March 1975 and took place just weeks after he had
scored his first international try against France in his penultimate
appearance.

In 1974 McBride led the then British Lions on a tour of South
Africa, a tour which was noted for the violence meted out by
provincial sides against the Lions. Known as 'The Invincibles',
the Lions won twenty-one of their twenty-two games, but cynical
violence overshadowed the tour. Tired of the physical abuse,
McBride came up with the '99 call' which was a signal that the
Lions players were to retaliate collectively to show their opponents
that they would not be bullied. The 99 call (which, it is claimed,
was supposed to be 999, but, given the mayhem which commenced,
the final number was never heard!) was used to great effect during
the third test against South Africa in Port Elizabeth on 13 July 1974.
Leading by two tests to none, the Lions had the series within their
grasp when, after some vicious tackles had been meted out, McBride
deemed it necessary to make the call, sparking off a bout of mass

fisticuffs that has gone down in history as 'The Battle of the Boet Erasmus Stadium'. With order restored eventually, the Lions went on to record a 26-9 victory, sealing the first home international series defeat for the Springboks in seventy-eight years. Afterwards a delighted McBride told the press, 'Now I can die happy, we did what we came to do.'

BRITISH OPEN CHAMPIONSHIP COMES TO PORTRUSH

Born in Portrush in 1911, Fred Daly became the first Irishman to win the Open Championship when he took honours at Royal Hoyelake in Liverpool in 1947. Daly's victory increased the pressure on the Royal and Ancient Golf Championship Committee to host the event in Northern Ireland and, in November 1949, it was announced that the championship would be held in Royal Portrush in 1951. The committee had travelled to view the facilities at both Royal County Down and Royal Portrush in October that year, but opted for the Antrim venue. The fact that Fred Daly was himself from the town was seen to be a decisive factor.

Founded as the County Club in 1888, the Portrush links were designed by 'Old' Tom Morris. In 1895 it was afforded 'Royal' Portrush Golf Club status when the Prince of Wales, the future King Edward VIII, became the club's patron. The course was redesigned in 1947 by the famous designer Harry Colt and hosted the qualifying rounds of the Open tournament, together with neighbouring Royal Portstewart, on 2 and 3 July 1951. Originally competitors from fourteen countries had entered the competition, but the late withdrawal of four of the leading Americans was met with 'indignation' by the organisers.

On the second day of competition, officials at the club were 'scandalised' when a Belfast bookmaker set up his board at the eighteenth green, shouting the odds and handing out tickets. The bookmaker was frogmarched off to a chorus of booing from the capacity crowd. Forty-six golfers qualified for the final round in a tournament that was won by Englishman Max Faulkner, who, for his on-course antics, had been christened 'The Clown Prince of Golfing'. Faulkner had worked on a farm the previous winter, milking cows to build up the power in his wrists, and won by two strokes in driving rain over second-placed Antonio Cerdá from Argentina. Faulkner took the top prize of £300, while hometown favourite Daly finished in joint fourth place, winning £62 10s for his endeavours.

THE ROYAL 'SPORT' OF COCKFIGHTING

In the days before it was outlawed, the 'Gentlemen of Antrim' had acquired a notable reputation in the 'sport' of cockfighting. On 9 February 1817, the Antrim gentry travelled to Dublin for a 'Grand Cock Match' against their counterparts from King's County (now Offaly) at the Cock Pit Royal in Essex Street, where winnings of 20 guineas a 'battle' and 1,000 guineas for the 'main battle' were the prizes on offer. In the *Belfast News Letter* of 25 February that year, a correspondent wrote that he could 'hardly believe that any number of gentlemen could be found in either of the counties mentioned, who could look on the distressed state of the poor at the present period, and at the same time devote a thousand guineas for the barbarous enjoyment of witnessing two cocks butcher each other with steel heels'. However, the sport remained the preserve of the landed gentry until it was outlawed in 1835, but still flourished in Ireland and in County Antrim in particular.

COCKFIGHTING FOILED BY RUC

Thirteen men from all over the Six Counties were charged at Ballyclare Petty Sessions yesterday with assisting at the fighting of gamecocks on 11 June. It was stated to be the first prosecution of its kind in County Antrim. Fines ranging from £15 to £25, and costs, were imposed, making a total of £275. Head Constable Montgomery told the Court that, accompanied by other police, he went to Glenhead by car, and drew up at the end of a long lane. He saw from 30 to 35 men there and several motor vehicles. On their arrival the men scattered in all directions, some carrying bags as they ran. The witness caught one man and afterwards seized 14 bags in the back of a van containing cocks. The witness suggested that the men were there for the purpose of fighting game cocks, to which the man he had captured retorted, 'Cock fighting should be legalised, the same as in other countries. It is no different than catching trout or shooting wild birds.' Sergeant Blackburn gave evidence that he had searched the surrounding area and found a rope ring with pegs and spade; also feathers, which appeared to come from fowl.

(*Irish Press*, 20 June 1958)

COUNTY ANTRIM AND DISTRICT FOOTBALL ASSOCIATION

The growth of association football in Ireland, especially in the North, was rapid and came under the auspices of the Irish Football Association after its foundation in 1880. Perhaps one of the heaviest trophies in world football is the Senior Shield, which has been organised by the County Antrim District and Football Association since 1889. The circular shield, which is mounted on a wooden frame, takes two men to lift when it is being presented. It was designed by Messrs Gibson & Co. of Belfast and has at its centre a medallion engraved with figures playing football. The medallion is surrounded by wreaths of oak and ivy leaves, together with twelve gold medals displaying harps, shamrocks, the monogram of the association and the arms of the Earl of Antrim.

It was considered to have been one of the greatest works ever produced by silversmiths in Belfast and is still played for by senior and junior clubs in north-east Ulster. The first final took place at the Ulster Ground in Belfast on 30 March 1889. Distillery were victorious as they put eight goals past YMCA, who responded with four. Distillery's captain, Billy Crone, was presented with the Senior Shield by the Lord Mayor of Belfast, Mr Charles C. Connor, in front of a crowd estimated at 5,000. Interestingly, Billy Crone was considered to have been the first-ever international manager when he took charge of Ireland in their 6-0 defeat to England at the Trent Bridge Cricket Ground on 20 February 1897.

BASKETBALL GLORY FOR ANTRIM

Although all-Ireland success in Gaelic games has so far eluded Antrim at senior county level, the county had the distinction of winning national basketball honours at both minor and senior levels in 1958. The senior final, against Roscommoh, was played on Saturday 10 May in front of a capacity crowd in Dublin's Cathal Brugha Barracks. Antrim were victorious on a 49-34 scoreline. Their English-born captain, Ken Davenport, was in fine form and put in a superb display of dribbling and accuracy to score the vital points. The northerners were described as 'superbly fit' as their stamina saw them home against the westerners. In the minor final earlier that evening, a virtuoso performance by Ray Mulholland helped Antrim to an easy win that was not reflected by the 29-18 final score.

The following year, Antrim relinquished their senior crown 29-26 to a Kilkenny side whose teamwork was the key to their success. There was consolation for the Antrim supporters who had travelled the long distance to the Marble City when the minors retained their title by beating Cork 31-20. In all, Antrim won the senior title, in what was a short-lived competition, on five occasions: in 1956, '58, '60, '63 and '64.

HARE COURSING IN ANTRIM

In Victorian times, hare coursing in Antrim was held at Massereene Park, in Antrim town. Many thousands descended on the home of Viscount Massereene to watch the ancient sport. Organised by the North Union Sporting Club, the meetings were overseen by the great and the good, with Lord Lurgan presiding as chief steward. In the 1920s, coursing moved to the Crebilly Club, based on the outskirts of Ballymena. As the public attitude to coursing changed, the annual Crebilly meeting on Boxing Day (St Stephen's Day) was to become the scene of violent protests, involving frequent clashes with the police. Despite the 'muzzling' of greyhounds in 1991, coursing declined in popularity and was banned in 2004 with the implementation of the Hunting Act at Westminster.

'ELECTRIC HARE COURSING' COMES TO IRELAND

Ireland's first-ever greyhound race meeting (originally known as electric hare coursing) took place at Celtic Park, Belfast, on the afternoon of Easter Monday, 18 April 1927. A curious crowd of 3,000 assembled to witness what was promoted as 'the greatest sport of its day' and saw Mr J.J. Tuite's 'Mutual Friend' take the honours in the first race. Celtic Park had been leased from the owners, Belfast Celtic Football Club, by the National Greyhound Racing Company, for the sum of £600 per annum. The 550-yard track was illuminated by eighty lights under which greyhounds chased a mechanical hare that ran at speeds of up to 60mph. It was a sport aimed specifically at the working classes, with 100 boarding kennels provided at the ground, which enabled owners to have their dogs trained, groomed and fed for £1 a week. Racing took place twice weekly in the evenings, 'when the working man is free from the toils and cares of the day', and was promoted as 'clean and exciting, without cruelty of any kind'. The sport proved to be a resounding success, with Shelbourne Park in Dublin opening its doors to dog racing in May that year, while Belfast's second venue at Dunmore Park opened in October. In December 1927, the greyhound franchise at Celtic Park was sold to the English-based National Greyhound Racing Association for the princely sum of £75,000. The last-ever greyhound race meeting was held at Celtic Park in November 1983.

However, in Ballymena, the growth of greyhound racing was frowned upon by many of a religious persuasion. When news emerged in 1933 that the County Antrim Agricultural Association had received an application to establish a track at its Ballymena Showgrounds, it sparked a protest by the Ballymena Church Council. The council expressed strong disapproval of any project that would 'encourage the terrible evil of betting and gambling'. The application was rejected.

DAVE 'BOY' MCAULEY

Dave 'Boy' McAuley was born in Larne in 1961 and during his professional career he held the IBF world title in the flyweight category. He was, pound for pound, arguably Ireland's greatest fighter over the past fifty years. His two epic fights against Fidel Bassa for the WBA Championship were both voted 'Fight of the Year', in 1987 and 1988 respectively. McAuley was a superb boxer who showed perhaps more bravery than any other modern Irish fighter. Anyone who was privileged enough to watch the Bassa fights would have witnessed a boxing masterclass – McAuley hauled himself off the canvas to go on and give Bassa the fright of his life. When McAuley finally defeated Duke McKenzie in 1989 for the IBF title, no Irish boxer deserved a world title more.

A FINE FIGHTING PEDIGREE

County Antrim can claim a total of nine Olympic boxing medals, with all of its successful boxers hailing from Belfast. In 1952, in Helsinki, John McNally became the first Irishman to claim a medal when he took silver in the bantamweight class. Four years later, in Melbourne, John Caldwell and Freddie Gilroy both won bronze medals, while in 1964, in Tokyo, Jim McCourt took bronze in the lightweight class. Hugh Russell from Belfast's New Lodge area won a bronze in Moscow in 1980 and as a professional would win the British title at both flyweight and bantamweight. Wayne McCullough, a future WBC World Champion, lost out in the 1992 bantamweight final in Barcelona. Paddy Barnes has the distinction of winning bronze medals at flyweight in both Beijing in 2008 and London in 2012. The list of County Antrim Olympic medals reached a grand total of nine when Michael Conlon took bronze in London in 2012 at flyweight.

THE SHANKILL ROAD
RECORD-BREAKER

Born in the Shankill Road district in May 1965, Norman Whiteside remains the only County Antrim-born footballer to score a winner in an FA Cup final. He fired home the decisive goal for Manchester United against Everton in May 1985. However, that feat was just one of a remarkable series of records set by Whiteside during the

1980s. Norman signed professional forms for United in 1982 and, in April that year, became the youngest debutante for the Red Devils since Duncan Edwards in 1953. In June he was the youngest-ever player to appear in a World Cup final series, when, at just 17 years and 41 days old, he surpassed Pele's record by appearing against Yugoslavia in Northern Ireland's opening game of the 1982 finals in Spain.

In 1983, he became the youngest goal scorer in the League Cup final, at 17 years and 323 days of age, when he hit the opening goal in United's 2-1 defeat by Liverpool. In that year's FA Cup final, after scoring the winner in the semi-final against Arsenal, he scored United's second goal against Brighton and Hove Albion when Manchester United won the replay 4-0, becoming the youngest player to score in the final of that competition. In a career cut short by injury, he scored sixty-eight goals in 278 League and Cup appearances for United, picking up two FA Cup winners medals.

SHAMROCKS FLY
THE FLAG FOR ANTRIM

In All-Ireland senior club hurling, Loughgiel Shamrocks have twice won national honours, firstly in 1983 and again in 2012. Their victory in 1983 came in a replay at Casement Park when they beat St Rynagh's of Offaly by 2-12 to 1-12. That year they had beaten Ballycastle in the Antrim final and disposed of Ballygalget of Down in the Ulster final. In the All-Ireland semi-final, the Ulster champions caused a sensation when they beat the Munster champions, Moycarkey Borris of Tipperary, by 2-7 to 1-6, thanks to goals from Aidan McCarry and Paddy Carey. The final at Croke Park on 17 April ended in a 2-5 to 1-8 draw, but the Antrim side edged home with a score of 2-12 to 1-12 in front of a crowd of 10,000 in the replay in Belfast a week later.

The Shamrocks' victory in the 2012 final in Dublin was due chiefly to the performance of one man: Liam Watson. The star forward scored 3-7 of Loughgiel's total when they saw off the challenge of Coolderry of Offaly on St Patrick's Day by 4-13 to 0-17. In the semi-final that year, the Shamrocks beat Limerick's

Na Piarsaigh 0-27 to 2-13. Watson racked up a total of 16 points for the Shamrocks in that match. The Shamrocks had qualified for that year's all-Ireland series when they claimed the Antrim title in 2011 with a win over Cushendall and the Ulster crown with an easy victory over Ballycran of Down. Five other Antrim teams have been runners-up in the competition: McQuillan's of Ballycastle in 1980, Belfast's O'Donovan Rossa in 1989, with Cushendall losing out to Limerick's Na Piarsaigh in 2016. However, Antrim's most unlucky team, Cú Chulainn's of Dunloy, have lost in four all-Ireland finals: 1995, 1996, 2003 and 2004.

TIPPERARY PREVAIL IN 1989 HURLING FINAL

On 3 September 1989, Antrim's hurlers appeared in only their second-ever All-Ireland senior hurling final when they faced a Tipperary side searching for their first title since 1971. Despite a famous semi-final win over Offaly, the Saffrons were rated as complete underdogs. The occasion soon began to take its toll on Antrim. Nicholas English led their defence on a merry dance as he totted up a record total of 2 goals and 12 points. A goal by Loughiel's Aidan McCarry early in the second half gave Antrim renewed hope, but the Premier County went up a gear and ended the game as the emphatic winners on a 4-24 to 3-9 scoreline. It was the largest winning margin in a final since Antrim's hurlers went down 5-16 to 0-4 to Cork in 1943 and was surpassed only when Waterford succumbed to Kilkenny on a 3-30 to 1-13 scoreline in 2008.

The county's most successful period came in the late 1980s and early 1990s. Five Saffron hurlers received All-Star awards during that period. They were Ciaran Barr (Rossa, Belfast) in 1988, Desy Donnelly (Ballycastle) and Olcan McFetridge (Armoy) in 1989, Terence McNaughten (Cushendall) in 1991 and Paul McKillen (Ballycastle) in 1993.

ANTRIM HURLERS HUMBLED BY DONEGAL

Antrim were not always the kingpins of hurling in Ulster, as the result of the 1907 Ulster final proved. The game saw Burt, the Donegal champions, host Carey Faughs of Antrim in Burt on Sunday 21 July, in a field at the foot of the famous O'Doherty castle. At least twenty carloads of Antrim supporters travelled from Derry city, while many hundreds of cyclists came from Strabane, Letterkenny and the Inishowen peninsula to see the game. The home supporters of Burt turned out in their masses to see the eagerly awaited tie. Such was the interest in the game that it was noted that there was a large turnout of the 'fair sex – more by far than we have ever seen at a match'.

Antrim suffered a setback before the game even commenced when three of their Belfast players failed to turn up and the Saffron side were forced to ask a Derry spectator to line out. Not surprisingly, Donegal's champions went about their task with great gusto on the grass, which, it was noted, was in 'need of a trim', building up a sizeable lead of 15 points to 1 at the break. The second half was a rout for Burt, who, through their talisman George Dowds, exposed the frailties of the Antrim backline, firing home 5 goals in the second half. The correspondent suggested that Donegal's fine win was down to their players' ability to play the game with the *camán* (hurley), as opposed to their tongues.

SAFFRONS' POOR SHOWING IN ULSTER CHAMPIONSHIP

A near-record crowd of 33,000 witnessed Antrim's last-ever Ulster senior football final victory when they defeated Cavan on 29 July 1951. The Saffrons, who had last held the crown in 1946, won the game by a single point (1-7 to 2-3) when Ray Beirne sent over the winner from a 30-yard free in the last minute. In the national semi-final that year, Antrim lost to Meath by two points at Croke Park, which was to be their last appearance in the latter stages of the all-Ireland senior football series. Antrim fans had to wait until 1970 to see their senior footballers in Ulster-final action again, when they lost to Derry by 4 points. However, football in Antrim went into a terminal decline during the Troubles and it wasn't until 2009 that the county appeared in the final again. That year they lost to reigning all-Ireland champions Tyrone by 1-18 to 0-15.

CARRICK RANGERS GIVE LINFIELD 'THE BLUES'

Perhaps the greatest upset in the history of the Irish Cup occurred on 10 April 1976 when 'B' Division Carrick Rangers humbled the mighty Linfield in the final at the Oval in Belfast. Led by player-manager Jimmy Brown, the junior club were victorious over 'The Blues' (2-1), thanks to a brace of goals from striker Gary Prenter. Carrick, under captain George Matchett, had fought their way through the preliminary rounds and had beaten first division sides Ballymena, Coleraine and Larne before reaching the showpiece final. On qualifying for the European Cup Winners' Cup competition, the Carrickfergus side beat Aris Bonnevoie of Luxembourg 4-3 on aggregate in their opening tie. Their dream run came to an end abruptly when English FA Cup holders Southampton beat them 9-3 over two legs in the second round. Established in 1939, Carrick Rangers were afforded top-flight status in Irish League football in 1983.

THE SKY BLUE 'BRAIDMEN'

Formed in April 1928, Ballymena FC (not to be confused with Ballymena United, who succeeded the club in 1934) made their League debut against Belfast Celtic at their Showgrounds in August that year. They rounded off a fantastic first season by winning the Irish Cup against Celtic at Cliftonville's Solitude ground on 30 March 1929. In front of a near-record 25,000 crowd, Celtic, the reigning league champions, took the lead in the twenty-fourth minute only for the Braidmen to battle back with goals from Jamie Shields and Jimmy 'Hoodie' McCambridge. The club had reached the final by defeating Glentoran, Broadway and Coleraine and the Irish Football Association awarded the side with a replica of the Cup in perpetuity in recognition of their feat. Ballymena were suspended from the Irish League in April 1934 for making illegal payments to amateur players and were replaced two months later by Ballymena United. The club has never won the Irish League title, but it has won the Irish Cup on six occasions: 1929, 1940, 1958, 1981, 1984 and 1989.

THE UNDISPUTED KING OF THE ROADS

The motorcycling world was left stunned on Sunday, 2 July 2000 when news broke of the death of sporting legend Joey Dunlop. The tragedy occurred when Joey was taking part in the 125cc race in Estonia's capital Tallinn. He was killed instantly when his bike skidded out of control on a rain-slick track and crashed into a tree. William Joseph Dunlop was a quiet, shy Ballymoney man, better known to his fans as 'Yer Man'. He was a true superstar in motorcycle racing – and that is an understatement. He was aged just 48 when he died and had spent decades competing at the very pinnacle of world road racing. In his long and successful career, Joey had won five Formula One World Championships and until his death he was still beating men half his age on the roads. The year 2000 was Joey's twenty-fifth year as a competitor. His feats at the Isle of Man TT races were exceptional. He shattered records and in that year's event he won his third career hat-trick – the Formula One, the 250cc and the 125cc races – bringing his total number of wins on the island to twenty-six. He was, quite simply, the 'King of the Roads'.

His worldwide fame and fortune never affected him and he was at his happiest behind his bar in Ballymoney, with his family or fixing one of his many bikes. He received an MBE in 1986 for his services to motorbike racing, which was followed in 1996 by an OBE for his humanitarian work for children in Romanian orphanages. Joey Dunlop was buried on Friday, 7 July 2000. Over 50,000 people turned out to pay their respects. The sheer scale of the turnout in a remote part of Antrim was difficult to grasp and mourners were visible as far as the eye could see. Joey's second cousin, Stanley Lee, was among the stewards at the service. He described the local community as devastated because they believed Joey to be just invincible. 'Part of Ballymoney has died too,' he said. 'We thought it would never happen.' On 15 May 2008, Joey's younger brother,

Robert, died tragically after suffering severe chest injuries in a crash during practice at the North West 200 near Portrush.

LIAM BECKETT – A RACONTEUR SUPREME

One of the best-known voices on Radio Ulster's sports coverage is the Ballymoney-born Liam Beckett. His punditry, delivered in his distinctive Ballymoney accent, is well-respected and his witticisms are priceless. Born William Alexander Beckett in 1951, his family called him Liam to distinguish him from all the 'Billys, Willys and Williams' who grew up around him. As a footballer, he played for Crusaders and Coleraine in the Irish League, as well as for Drogheda in the League of Ireland, before moving into management with Ballymoney United, Cliftonville and then Institute. On signing for Drogheda United, club officials, assuming that he was a Catholic with a name like Liam, brought him up to see the head of St Oliver Plunkett for luck and inspiration. However, embarrassed officials soon discovered that they had made the wrong assumption, as Liam recalled, 'I had as much interest in his [Oliver Plunkett's] head as he had in mine, but the penny dropped that they didn't know I was a Protestant.'

When his football career came to an end, Beckett teamed up with the Dunlop brothers and for twenty years he worked as a mechanic and a manager to Robert until his untimely death in 2008. Beckett's wit sets him apart as a commentator of note. On one occasion, on observing a Linfield footballer sending a wayward pass to a forward, he commented, 'He couldn't find Black Beauty in a field of white daisies.' Another quip concerned a similar less-than-accurate pass; Beckett observed, 'He couldn't pass you a sandwich at a wake.' Liam's autobiography, *Full Throttle: Robert Dunlop, Road Racing and Me*, was published in May 2016.

ROAD RACING AT DUNDROD

The road-racing circuit on the outskirts of Belfast at Dundrod has attracted tens of thousand fans over the years and is today the home of the Ulster Grand Prix bike races. The 7-mile circuit snakes along narrow country roads and was the venue for the RAC Tourist Trophy race for motor cars between 1950 and 1955. The event was one part of the FIA World Sports Championship. However, in September 1955, the occasion was marred by accidents which claimed the lives of three competitors and led effectively to the end of motor racing at the circuit. The races took place within three months of the infamous incident at the Le Mans circuit in France, when eighty-three spectators were killed by a car that careered into the crowd. There had been calls for the Dundrod event to be cancelled in light of this, but organisers had been confident that enough safety measures had been put in place.

The races, which took place on Saturday 17 September, were held in damp weather conditions, but this did not stop the spectators from turning out in force. On the previous day, Stirling Moss had set a new lap record of almost 93mph during official practice. However, the first death occurred at the Cochranestown's part of the course when 26-year-old Londoner Jack Mayers was killed instantly when his Cooper burst into flames on hitting a bank. Crowds watched in horror as 21-year-old Bill Smith of Lincoln died when his Connaught car thundered into the flaming debris. Despite the accident, racing continued, but three hours later Richard Mainwaring met his death when his car exploded and burst into flames after overturning at Tornagrough.

The inquests into the fatalities took place in Lisburn and returned verdicts of 'accidental death'. Stirling Moss, the joint winner of the race, told the inquest that, in his view, too many inexperienced drivers had taken part in the event. He added, 'Every driver in an event of this standard should be vetted for racing skill, knowledge of car and racing experience. I would rather drive neck and neck with [Juan Manuel] Fangio and Mike Hawthorn than try to pass some of the less experienced drivers.' Despite the traumatic events, Charles Gordon Neill, secretary of the Ulster Automobile Association, denied that the future of the race would be jeopardised by the deaths. 'We could reasonably expect a bigger entry next year, and a bigger attendance – accidents encourage the public to come,' he told the *Irish Press*. He added, 'All day hundreds of people drove from Belfast to the course to see the scene of the crashes.' In April 1956, the RAC announced that it had decided to postpone the event at Dundrod that year. The race would not to take place again until 1958, when purpose-built courses had been constructed in England at Goodwood, Oulton Park, Silverstone and Donnington Park.

THE FABULOUS
ANTHONY PETER (AP) MCCOY

Born in Moneyglass in 1974, Anthony Peter McCoy – better known
as 'AP' to racing aficionados – remains the most successful jockey
in the history of jump racing. He learned his trade as a boy under
the watchful eye of family friend Willie Rock in Cullybackey.
At the age of 15, he began his apprenticeship in Carlow under Jim
Bolger's strict regime, where smoking and drinking were banned
and going to Mass on Sunday was compulsory. McCoy earned just
£100 a week. He rode his first winner, Legal Steps, at Thurles in
1992, but back then no one considered him to be a future champion.
Everything changed in January 1993, when he had a horrific fall
on frozen ground. His leg break was so severe that McCoy could
not ride for five months, but the time spent recuperating made the
fledgling jockey ask serious questions about what he wanted from
life. He resolved to be the greatest jockey of all time.

After a career that spanned 17,630 rides, he retired in April 2015.
He rode 4,348 winners in Britain and Ireland and won twenty
consecutive Champion Jump Jockey titles. His first win in England
was on the Gordon Edwards-trained Chickabiddy at Exeter in
September 1994. McCoy's final winner was Capard King at Ayr on
17 April, his twenty-sixth winner since announcing his retirement.
He won the King George VI Chase on Best Mate in 2002 and, after
fifteen years of trying, won the Grand National aboard Don't Push
It in 2010. His 289 winners in 2001–02 beat Sir Gordon Richards'
record of 269. He won the Cheltenham Gold Cup on two occasions,
on Mr Mulligan in 1997 and on Synchronised in 2011. He followed
that up with three Champion Hurdle victories. In 2003 McCoy was
awarded an MBE in the Queen's Birthday Honours and an OBE
followed in 2010. That year he also became the first jockey to be
voted BBC Sports Personality of the Year, beating Phil Taylor and
Jessica Ennis-Hill.

However, for all the sporting superlatives, it is the monastic
lifestyle that McCoy led throughout his career that made him a
superstar. While his natural weight was about 11st 6lbs and he stood
at 5ft 10in, McCoy reduced his weight to 10st in order to compete.
At breakfast, he was said to suck on ice cubes to stave off the hunger
that remained after his one slice of dry toast. Lunch was either a few
Jelly Babies or a Jaffa Cake with tea. Dinner was usually steamed
fish or chicken and vegetables. On three nights of the week he went

without dinner. In all, he suffered twice from punctured lungs, broke both shoulder blades and thirteen other bones, and had teeth chipped on fourteen occasions. Like all great jockeys, he took a matter-of-fact view of the dangers of his sport. 'I've always been prepared to get injured. It's not something that bothers me. I'm a jump-jockey. I will end up in that ambulance from time to time.'

6

AN ENTERTAINING HERITAGE

CALL MY BROTHER BACK – MICHAEL MCLAVERTY

Michael McLaverty was born in 1904 in Carrickmacross, County Monaghan. His book *Call My Brother Back* is a superb evocation of life on Rathlin Island and then in Belfast during the early part of the 1920s. McLaverty spent part of his own early childhood on Rathlin and was educated at St Malachy's College and Queen's University of Belfast. Written in 1939, the book begins amid the tranquillity of Rathlin and tells the story of Colm MacNeill, whose family make a poor living from the land and sea. The book recounts the simple life perfectly and tells how Colm won a scholarship to St Malachy's College in Belfast as a boarder. He lived with his older brother and sister in Belfast, but life in the city during the Troubles was hugely different to life on the island. Rathlin was isolated and rural whereas Belfast was enduring serious trouble, which coincided with the partition of Ireland.

The death of Colm's father on the island forced the rest of the family to move to Belfast and the story recounts the hardships they endured. It is a coming-of-age novel and is considered one of the finest first novels by an Irish writer. The Belfast he describes reflects the troubled times during which terror walked by night and morning revealed murder most foul. While the young McNeill strives to complete his education, his brother joins the IRA and his murder forms the tragic climax of the story.

McLaverty was not to make a fortune from the novel. In 1958, he was appointed the inaugural principal at St Thomas' School in Belfast. One of his trainee teachers in the early years was a Queen's

English graduate named Seamus Heaney. Heaney was greatly influenced by McLaverty and penned a book entitled *A Tribute to Michael McLaverty*, which was published by Belfast's Linen Hall Library in 2005.

'THE GREEN GLENS OF ANTRIM'

Far across yonder blue lies a true fairy land
With the sea rippling over the shingle and sand
Where the gay honeysuckle is luring the bee
And the green glens of Antrim are calling to me.

Written by Kenneth North, this striking ballad celebrates the beauty of the Nine Glens of Antrim. It has been recorded by numerous artists, most notably Eileen Donaghy, Ruby Murray, the Wolfe Tones, Bridie Gallagher and Daniel O'Donnell.

BACK TO THE FUTURE'S ANTRIM LINK

The village of Dunmurry, 6 miles west of Belfast, was the location for the ill-fated DeLorean factory from 1980 to 1982. John Zachery DeLorean was a high-flying executive with General Motors who formed his own company, persuading the then British government to support him by giving him the sum of almost £80 million to produce his gull-winged sports car. With unemployment levels in west Belfast at crisis levels, the establishment of the factory was a bold move in an area suffering the worst of the Troubles. Production began in 1981 and soon the workforce reached almost 2,600 as the stainless-steel cars rolled off the production line. Before long, the reality became a nightmare as less than 3,000 models were sold and redundancies were enforced. Despite seeming like an eternal optimist, DeLorean was facing a financial crisis and was arrested in a sting operation in October 1982 for his part in a drugs-linked money-laundering operation. An acutely embarrassed British government finally acted

a month later and closed the factory, leaving masses of unsold stock. Ironically, the sports car was to become an icon in 1985, when the *Back to the Future* films featured it as a time machine. However, for the bitter and unemployed workforce in Belfast, the car's 'rebirth' was too little, too late.

RATHLIN'S MUSICAL HERITAGE

Kevin Black, the father of the famous Black sisters, Mary and Frances, was born in the townland of Glacklugh on Rathlin Island in 1909. An accomplished musician, Kevin was well known as a piper, a fiddler and mandolin player of note on Rathlin and throughout the Glens of Antrim. In 1935, Kevin, a plasterer by trade, moved to Dublin's Charlemont Street, where he met Patricia (Patty) Daly, whom he married in 1949. The Black family spent their summer holidays on the island and it is still close to their hearts. On her 2003 album *How High the Moon*, Frances Black celebrated her father's birthplace in song with 'Rachra Island', the Irish name for Rathlin.

THE DAMAGED DARK HEDGES

The beautiful stretch of approximately 150 beech trees located at the Bregagh Road near Armoy have become world-famous as the site of the 'King's Road' from the hit series *Game of Thrones*. The enchanted tunnel of intertwining trees was planted by the Stuart family in 1775 to provide a charming approach to their Georgian residence, Gracehill House, which is now a golf club. The trees are one of the most photographed landmarks in County Antrim and have attracted thousands of *Game of Thrones* fans to the area. However, in late January 2016, the famous site was damaged by Storm Gertrude, which swept across Northern Ireland, uprooting two of the ancient beech trees. A week later, fans of the television show were up in arms about road contractors 'accidentally' painting white lines along the middle of the road, bringing a modern-day touch to the fairy-tale road. Flustered officials quickly admitted their

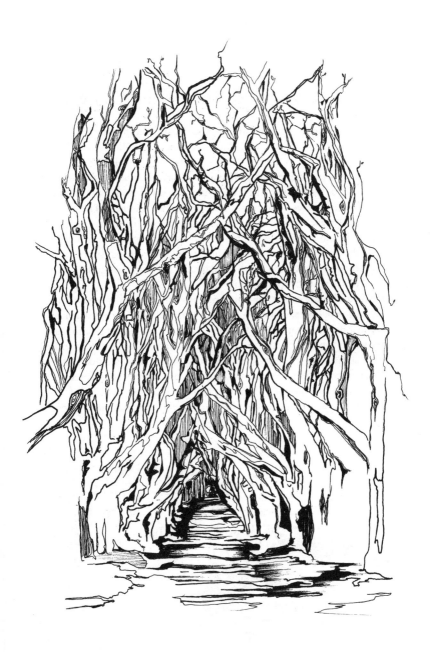

error and workmen were dispatched to the site post-haste to undo their erroneous handiwork.

COASTAL INSPIRATION FOR C.S. LEWIS

The picturesque ruins of Dunluce Castle, situated dramatically on a rocky outcrop of the north Antrim coast, were believed to be the inspiration for C.S. Lewis' castle Cair Paravel. This fantasy castle was first mentioned in his 1950 classic, *The Lion, the Witch and the Wardrobe*, which is the best known of the seven books that make up the Chronicles of Narnia. In the book, Lewis writes, 'The castle of Cair Paravel on its little hill towered up above them; before them were the sands, with rocks and little pools of saltwater, and seaweed, and the smell of the sea, and long lines of bluish green waves breaking forever and ever on the beach. And oh, the cry of the sea-gulls! Have you heard it? Can you remember?'

As a child, Lewis spent his holidays on the Antrim coast and visited many sites, including Dunluce Castle. His home at Little Lea in east Belfast afforded inspirational views across Belfast Lough and onwards towards the Antrim hills. The clifftop at Dunluce still seems like something straight out of a fantasy world. Lewis' books have been translated into dozens of languages and have been adapted for television and the stage. In 2005, the *The Lion, the Witch and the Wardrobe* was made into a film starring Tilda Swinton and James

McAvoy. It was a tremendous box-office success and the third most successful grossing film of 2005.

Clive Staple Lewis was born in Belfast on 29 November 1898. The death of his mother Florence in 1907 impacted greatly on the young author, who was sent as a boarder to Wynyard School in Watford. He died a week before his sixty-fifth birthday, on 22 November 1963. However, the news of his death was lost in the media frenzy that accompanied the assassination of US President J.F. Kennedy.

THE BEATLES COME TO TOWN

On Friday, 8 November 1963, Belfast's Great Victoria Street came to a standstill as thousands of screaming fans gathered in the hope of catching a glimpse of the world-famous pop group, the Beatles. Almost 100 police officers were called out to calm the teenagers who had congregated outside the ABC Ritz Cinema where the group were making their first Belfast appearance. Traffic was diverted from the area and two ambulances stood by in anticipation. The Beatles had slipped quietly into Belfast during the afternoon after evading a near riot on Thursday evening in Dublin. At the border they were met by a RUC patrol car and escorted to Belfast. About twenty uniformed and plain-clothes police saw them safely into the Ritz by a back door while about 100 young people, mostly schoolchildren, screamed outside. Inside, a lucky few were afforded a meet-and-greet with the group and John, Paul, George and Ringo were each presented with lucky shillelaghs by Miss Ann McGowan of Cregagh, near Belfast, chair of their Irish fan club.

By late afternoon the crowd outside had grown significantly. At one stage the teenagers rushed the doors and six girls fainted when rumours spread that the band were about to leave the arena. The police forced the crowd back and erected metal barriers, making a gangway to allow the 2,000 audience members in the cinema to leave. Soon the moment the crowd had waited for came and the group appeared. Amid a crescendo of screaming teenagers, the Beatles emerged and police fought to get them safely into their cars. Five people, including two young girls, were injured in the crush, while one man received a severe cut to his head as he was forced over the barrier. More crash barriers were placed outside the Grand Central Hotel in Royal Avenue where the Beatles stayed overnight and the fans kept up a constant wave of emotional screaming. The police had labelled the operation to preserve the peace as 'Beat the Beatlemania'.

During the mayhem, both people and property were harmed. Three months later, Mr George Lackie received over £140 in damages from the Belfast Corporation. In the Belfast Recorders Court, it was reported that some of the 2,000 crowd outside the Beatles' hotel had stood on his £2,000 Lancia car, hoping to get a better view of the Liverpool superstars. Later at the court, representatives of J. and W.F. Burrowes, merchants of Royal Avenue, were awarded a similar sum against the Corporation for a plate-glass window that was broken by crowds rushing to see the group.

BALLYMENA'S FAMOUS FLAMINGO BALLROOM

Opened in 1959 by Sammy Barr, the Flamingo Dance Hall in Ballymena's Ballymoney Street played host to some of the greatest names in popular music during the 1960s. As well as legends such as The Hollies, Pink Floyd, Tom Jones and Roy Orbison, American country singer 'Gentleman' Jim Reeves played to a packed audience at the hall on 19 June 1963. That appearance was part of a whistle-stop tour of Ireland, which saw Reeves perform later that evening at the Royal Arms Ballroom in Omagh, County Tyrone. Reeves was a perfectionist who had refused to appear at two previous engagements because he felt the pianos at the venues were not up to scratch. However, Gentleman Jim was so delighted by the sound produced by the piano in the Flamingo that he went out of his way to thank Sammy Barr publicly before his encore. Indeed, he asked the owner if he could borrow the piano for the remainder of his tour. Just over a year later, on 31 July 1964, Jim Reeves died in an air crash while on his way to Nashville. That very night in the Flamingo Dance Hall, the Rolling Stones were appearing just one week after their single 'It's All Over Now' had topped the British charts. The hall closed in 1980 when it was bought by the Wellington Street Presbyterian Church.

LED ZEPPELIN'S ANTRIM LINKS

The atmospheric photograph on the front cover of Led Zeppelin's fifth studio album *The Houses of the Holy* was taken at the Giant's Causeway. The cover depicts undressed children climbing on the basalt columns and the cover was actually banned in the United States and Spain. The inside fold-out sleeve of the 1973 album is adorned with a picture of nearby Dunluce Castle. That is not the only link that the legendary rock band has to Antrim. On 5 March 1971, the crowd in Belfast's Ulster Hall witnessed the band playing the first-ever live version of their all-time classic 'Stairway to Heaven'.

LIAM NEESON'S EARLY PROMISE

The 1971 Mid-Ulster Drama Festival, which was held in Carrickmore, County Tyrone, was considered to have been of a particular high standard. The proceedings were adjudicated by Lisle Jones, a well-known London drama personality, who noted, in particular, the performance of a young Ballymena actor. The Slemish Players were praised for their production of Brian Friel's *The Lovers*, with Liam Neeson receiving mentions in dispatches for his 'versatility and mimicry skills' when playing the part of Joe. In Larne the previous year, 18-year-old Neeson had won the gold medal for his performance as Joe at the festival and had been noted as 'one for the future' by correspondents.

Born in Ballymena in 1952, Liam Neeson was a boxer and hurler in his youth and dabbled in acting while at primary school. In the early 1970s, he attended Belfast's Queen's University but left to take up a job at Guinness. In 1976, he joined the Lyric Players in Belfast and made his screen debut a year later, playing Christ in *The Pilgrim's Progress*. In 1993, he was nominated for the best actor accolade at that year's Oscars ceremony. His other screen credits include the 1996 film *Michael Collins*, *Star Wars* and the *Taken* trilogy. In 2000, he declined the freedom of his home town of Ballymena as some councillors had objected to comments he had made about historical anti-Catholic sectarianism in the town. However, in 2013, he accepted the honour and sat beside Ian Paisley and his wife Eileen at the civic dinner to mark the occasion. Ironically, Neeson in his youth had been impressed by Ian Paisley as an orator and claimed that he had been inspired to become an actor after witnessing the 'Big Mary' performance.

RICHARD HAYWARD – THE MAN WHO BROUGHT HOLLYWOOD TO GLYNN

Born in Southport, near Liverpool, in 1892, Richard Hayward settled in Larne, where he became a poet, actor, singer and archaeologist of note. He made records with Belfast comedian Jimmy O'Dea and played the dour northerner to O'Dea's ebullient Dubliner in the 1935 film *The Luck of the Irish*. The film was based on Colonel Victor Haddick's novel of the same name and its outdoor scenes were shot in the picturesque village of Glynn, near Larne. Many locals were used as extras during filming as the village was transformed into a Hollywood set. Local man James Patton, who was a child at the time, remembers how the excitement, 'There were lorries everywhere, with giant lights, and camera crews were everywhere, it was just pandemonium.' Hayward wrote a song entitled 'The Humour is now on Me', which was also used in *The Quiet Man*, and he made an appearance in the classic 1950s portrayal of the sinking of the *Titanic*, *A Night to Remember*. He also discovered the English actress Dinah Sheridan and launched her career when he cast her in *Irish and Proud* at the age of just 15. She went on to appear in *The Railway Children* and with Kenneth More in the 1953 British comedy *Genevieve*.

Staying faithful to the east Antrim coast, Hayward's next film, *The Early Bird*, was filmed in Glenarm and Carnlough. It broke box-office records in parts of Ireland and attracted critical acclaim. A prominent member of the Orange Order, Hayward died tragically in a car crash near Ballymena on 13 October 1964, aged 72.

MY LADY OF THE CHIMNEY CORNER

Alexander Irvine was born in Antrim town in January 1863 to Anna and Jamie Irvine. The family of eleven moved to nearby Crumlin, where they endured a life of austere poverty and hardship. As a young man, Alexander worked in the coal mines of Scotland before joining the navy and eventually won a scholarship to Oxford University. He was ordained a minister and then travelled to New York where he worked among the poor in the Bowery district. He served in the trenches during the First World War and on returning to the United States was elected to the National Executive of the American Socialist Party.

Irvine was, though, a County Antrim man at heart and would never forget his impoverished upbringing close to Lough Neagh. In 1913, he wrote the classic *My Lady of the Chimney Corner*, which was an enthralling account of nineteenth-century Ireland. The 'Lady' in the book is his mother, Anna, who struggled to bring up her family. The book vividly outlines life before, during and after the potato famine and is set in Pogue's Entry in Antrim town. It tells the tale of a couple who entered a mixed marriage and how they battled austerity, sharing their nettle soup with their neighbours on Sundays. But warmth and positivity are at the core of the story, which recounts how the family survived and thrived – the guiding belief of the book is that love will conquer all and achieve wonders in adversity. Irvine was 78 when he died in California in 1941.

In 1927, a stone was erected in Antrim parish church in memory of Alexander's mother Anna and father Jamie. Seven years later, a ceremony, presided over by the Viscount Massereene and Ferrard, dedicated the cottage and an inscribed golden key was used to formally open 'The Chimney Corner'. Mrs Mary Scott, Alexander's sister, placed on the tombstone of their mother and father, in the Antrim churchyard, a wreath with the inscription, 'In remembrance of an Irishman and Irish woman whose light still shines'.

Despite these early attempts to preserve the cottage, in the 1950s a Scottish visitor complained to Antrim Rural Council that the cottage was in a state of disrepair. He received a terse response stating that 'the matter was of no concern of the Council'. The clerk, Mr K.R. Holden, said that the council's solicitor had recommended that no action be taken in the matter. In 1963, the dilapidated house in Pogue's Entry was bought by a group of friends and admirers of Irvine with the intention of creating a tourist attraction. The cottage was restored to its original state and today it stands at the junction of Castle Way and Church Street.

ANGELA'S ASHES –
THE MCCOURTS OF MONEYGLASS

The publication of Frank McCourt's classic *Angela's Ashes* in 1996 brought fame to the village of Moneyglass, near Toome, where Frank's father Malachy was born in 1900. Malachy McCourt was a son of Francis and Mary McCourt and, as the author recalled, 'he [Malachy] grew up wild, in trouble with the English, or the Irish, or both. He fought with the Old IRA and for some desperate act he wound up a fugitive with a price on his head.' Malachy, according to the book, was secreted out of Ireland to New York, where 'with Prohibition in full swing, he thought he had died and gone to hell for his sins. Then he discovered speakeasies and he rejoiced.' He married Angela Sheehan from Limerick but the family soon returned to Ireland where they stayed for a short period at the McCourt family farm in Moneyglass. After travelling to Limerick via Dublin, the family settled in the lanes of the city, where the tale of poverty continued. During the war, Malachy went to work near Coventry, but again alcoholism took hold and the family was left penniless back in Limerick. In August 1985, Malachy McCourt died and was buried in Belfast, after spending his final days 'drinking tea with the ladies of Andersonstown'. The book was published when Frank was 66 and won a Pulitzer Prize. It was turned into a Hollywood movie, directed by Alan Parker and starring Emily Watson and Robert Carlyle, whose portrayal of Malachy and his County Antrim accent was well received.

7

A RELIGIOUS AND PIOUS LEGACY

NO HURLING ON A SUNDAY IN CLOUGHMILLS

The prospect of Cloughmills' hurlers hosting close rivals Loughiel in their village on Sunday, 22 April 1945 incurred the wrath of local sabbatarians, who were none too pleased at the prospect. On the Friday before the game, a mob went on the rampage in the village, smashing the windows in twenty Catholic homes as well as those at the home of local priest, Father Vincent Leonard. The stones had been wrapped in letters which condemned anyone who would 'disrespect the Lord's Day'. The following morning it was discovered that the hurling field had been vandalised. The goalposts had been cut down and a placard had been erected at the entrance gate, stating, 'This is for Vincent Leonard and the hurlers – RIP'. The game went ahead regardless, with a heavy police presence in attendance. Loughiel were reported to have won the game.

SAFFRON GAELS TOLD TO AVOID 'CORRUPT' ENGLISH SPORT

In May 1931, Sean McKeown, secretary of the County Antrim Board of the GAA, delivered a strongly worded attack on any Gael who had the audacity to support 'soccer football'. Addressing the county convention at the McAllister Hall in Ballycastle, McKeown accused those who played or attended soccer games of 'acting as traitors to the cause of independence, helping to put Ireland into a civilisation which England wanted to impose'. He added that soccer was 'surrounded by rottenness and corruption and any man who paid to watch it was worse than the man who played it, because he was keeping up what was really a bad business, which was below sport'. As an alternative, he strongly advocated that delegates take up Irish dancing, remarking that it was a healthy pastime, whereas jazz music, he suggested, lowered both one's vitality and mentality.

Ironically, at the following year's convention in Cushendun, McKeown criticised those who made attempts to link the GAA with politics. He claimed that the GAA was a non-political organisation and stated that the organisation must continue to 'keep a straight course in this matter'. McKeown had, by 1940, assumed the position of chairman of the Antrim board. At that year's convention, delegates passed a further motion, perhaps appreciated by Mr McKeown, which stated 'that any member of the Association known to attend foreign dances would be expelled'.

OPPOSITION TO THE DUNLOY SUNDAY PICTURE HOUSE

Hurling was not the only pursuit which received sabbatarian ire in north Antrim in the 1950s. In Dunloy, the prospect of a cinema opening on a Sunday compelled many to write to Antrim County Council, fuming with self-righteous anger at the prospect. 'Our religious sentiments are outraged,' said Revd J.H. Brown, Moderator of Dunloy Presbyterian church, in a letter to the council. 'After all, Antrim isn't Kerry. Protestants will regard this [a cinema opening on a Sunday] as an abomination which will almost lead to a breach of the peace,' added the clergyman. Complaining that the sanctity of the Sabbath in Dunloy was already being desecrated by 'Roman Catholic neighbours buzzing and bellowing in their sports on a Sunday,' Revd Brown suggested that it would not be long before a dreaded greyhound track would open in the village. The secretary of the council, who had read out the letter, pointed out that nothing could be done since the decision to permit the cinema to open on a Sunday had been unanimous. The council took no action.

AMALGAMATION OF SCHOOLS – OPPOSITION FROM ON HIGH

In January 1935, a resolution of protest was passed at a meeting of Catholic residents in Ballycastle against a government-led policy of amalgamating Catholic boys' and girls' schools. The protest meeting had been convened by the local parish priest, Father John McAleese, who said the Ministry of Education was endeavouring to implement a policy which was totally at odds with Catholic teaching. He advised the audience that the Catholic Church believed that boys and girls required different training to equip them for their roles in life. In a comment that was crass in the extreme, the priest stated that 'Catholic children were more intelligent than those of other denominations'. This, he added, was not just his opinion, but also the view of a Protestant school inspector, who had told him 'that the children at Catholic schools were brighter and more intelligent than the children at Protestant schools'. If the priest's comments had not been insensitive enough, Father McAleese further stated that the inspector had told him that Catholic children were more intelligent as their families did not permit near relations to marry. 'Other Churches,' added McAleese, 'allowed marriage to a near relation, and the result was that the children were degenerate and often stupid.'

DEAN SWIFT'S ANTRIM COTTAGE DESTROYED – 1959

Jonathan Swift, author of *Gulliver's Travels*, was born in Hoey's Court, Dublin, on 30 November 1667. His first ministerial appointment in 1694 was to the parish of Kilroot in the Diocese of Connor. He stayed in Antrim for just over a year and, on resigning, returned to Oxford, where he began the first phase of his successful career in literature. At Kilroot, Swift proposed to a local tanner's daughter, Jane Waring, whom he called Varina, but his affections were spurned, much to his disappointment. Correspondence from Swift survives in which he offers to remain in Kilroot if Varina would marry him, promising to leave and never return to Ireland if she refused. In Kilroot, his congregation was small and indifferent to the new clergyman. He recounted how he would go to the shore and skip stones by the sea and 'when sufficient idlers came to watch, he swept them up and carried them off to church'. Dean Swift's former cottage at Kilroot was destroyed by fire in 1959. It had been occupied until 1957.

THE GREAT RELIGIOUS REVIVAL OF 1859

The Great Religious Revival of 1859 in Antrim can be traced back to the United States. The *Irish Presbyterian* reported in June 1858, that, 'A revival is now passing over the churches of America such has not been known since apostolic times'. That revival had been inspired in part by Ulster Protestant immigrants. The movement in Ulster – and Antrim in particular – can be traced back to Dr William Gibson and Revd William McClure, who spread their crusading message after witnessing the American 'awakening' at first hand. The Baptist Minister, J. Edwin Orr, described the events of 1859 as a revival 'which originated in a prayer meeting of four young men in the village school house of Kells, and made a greater impact spiritually on Ireland, than anything else known since the days of St. Patrick'. By the spring of 1859, also known as 'The Year of Grace', the growth in prayer meetings had swept with great zeal across the Antrim area.

In Portrush, hundreds of 'lost souls' were converted to the word of God, while 'several Roman Catholics had vowed not to return to mass and priest no more'. In November 1859, an English visitor to County Antrim reported that 'drunkenness, swearing and fornication had greatly decreased' and, in Crumlin, ten of the town's sixteen bars had not applied for the renewal of their liquor licences. In October, the Ballymoney Quarter Sessions reported that no cases were to be heard and this was seen as a direct consequence of the revival. Stories of people fainting and having visions at open-air prayer meetings abounded.

'IT'S A KNOCKOUT' FOR REVD IAN PAISLEY

The decision of Carrickfergus Council to permit the BBC to film a heat of its popular show *It's a Knockout* on Sunday, 23 April 1978 incurred the wrath of the Free Presbyterian Church, who turned up to protest against the 'latest desecration of the Sabbath Day'. Led by Revd Ian Paisley, the 'big man' condemned the event 'as the latest Republican plot between the BBC and the town councillors [of Carrickfergus] to reduce the Protestant Sabbath to a continental Roman Sunday'. As teams from Carrickfergus, Dungannon and Derry battled for supremacy, the 4,000 spectators arriving were greeted with banners proclaiming, 'It's a Holy Day, Not a Holiday' and 'Your Sins Will Find You Out'.

Paisley was unrepentant, telling reporters that the BBC was anti-Protestant since it chose not to hold the event while local Catholics had been attending Mass at 10 p.m. that morning. The BBC, however, dismissed any claims that the holding of the event on a Sunday was anti-Protestant, pointing out that it had filmed a heat of the series on a Sunday in Bangor, County Down, in 1968, when no objectors had turned up to protest. Interestingly, despite serving as the MP for North

Antrim for many decades and despite his close affinity with Ballymena, Ian Paisley was born in Armagh in 1926. He lived the majority of his life in Ballyhackamore on the outskirts of east Belfast, which is actually in County Down.

CARDINAL CATHAL DALY

Born in Loughgiel in 1917, Cathal Brendan Daly's family lived a penny-wise and devout life. He is remembered for being a man of great intellect, for his uncompromising Catholic conservatism and for his strident criticisms of paramilitaries. From an early age it seemed that Dr Daly was destined for the priesthood. He studied at St Malachy's College in Belfast, read classics at the Queen's University and then enrolled at Maynooth, where he was ordained in June 1941. He spent twenty-one years as a lecturer in the Scholastic Philosophy Department at Queen's University until he was appointed Bishop of Ardagh and Clonmacnoise in 1967. His work carried out behind the scenes as an adviser to Irish Church authorities marked him out as a thinker and a diplomat. When Pope John Paul II visited Ireland in 1979, Daly drafted the famous plea for peace which the pontiff delivered at Drogheda.

When Cardinal Tomás Ó Fiaich died in 1990, Cathal Daly, at the age of 73, succeeded him as Archbishop of Armagh and Primate of All Ireland. He was a principled leader but was attacked from many sides. Republicans accused him of being pro-British. Ian Paisley called him the 'black Pope of the republican movement' while another clergyman dubbed him the 'red-hatted weasel'. His time as cardinal coincided with some of the greatest upheavals in the Irish Catholic Church. He led the onslaught against Charles Haughey's plans to legalise contraception and was in office as the avalanche of clerical sexual abuse scandals swamped Ireland. After his retirement in 1996, Dr Daly returned to reading and writing in his home in south Belfast. He published his autobiography in 1998, omitting the scandals that marred the last years of his tenure as Primate of All Ireland. Several other books followed and he continued writing, travelling and speaking at events well into his 80s, despite a long-standing heart condition.

He died in a Belfast hospital in January 2010, aged 92. Despite their previously fraught relationship, Republicans remembered him warmly in their tributes. Martin McGuinness acknowledged that while there was no love lost between Sinn Féin and the cardinal during the Troubles, they had several warm encounters in later years. The tributes to Dr Daly which poured in included warm words from Alan Harper, Church of Ireland Primate, who praised him as a fearless champion of peace and justice, who was always speaking out unambiguously on community issues during the darkest days of the Troubles.

ST PATRICK'S FOOTPRINT

Overlooking Ballymena, Slemish Mountain was believed to be the first home of St Patrick in Ireland. According to folklore, Patrick was brought to Antrim as a slave and worked as a shepherd on the slopes of the mountain for Milchu. For a period of six years, Patrick suffered from homesickness and loneliness. Yearning for home, he turned to prayer. While in the grounds of nearby the Skerry church, he saw what he believed to be his guardian angel (Victor), who told Patrick to escape and return home. The vision was recorded in verse by St Fiech, who wrote:

> Victor said to Milchu's slave
> Go thou over the sea

> He placed his foot upon a stone
> Its trace remains and wears not away.

St Patrick's footprint is said to be indented in a stone close to the churchyard. Patrick did escape but on becoming a priest he returned to Ireland to convert his old master. The rest, as they say, is history.

Slemish Mountain, which is actually a volcanic plug, reaches a height of 437 metres above the surrounding plain. It is a popular walking destination and each St Patrick's Day thousands climb to the top of the mountain in pilgrimage. The mountain's summit affords spectacular views of the Antrim and Scottish coasts, Lough Neagh and the Sperrin Mountains.

8

FAMINE, HUNGER
AND HARDSHIP

THE GREAT FROST 1740–1741

Ireland – and Ulster and Antrim in particular – was affected greatly
by 'The Great Frost' which occurred between December 1739
and September 1741. The year 1740 was known as '*bliain an áir*'
(the year of slaughter) and the cold snap was thought to have been
caused by a volcanic eruption in the Kamchatka peninsula in Russia
that pumped tons of smoke, dust and ash into the upper atmosphere.
During the period, Lough Neagh froze over and there are many
stories of people being able to travel by foot from Antrim to Tyrone
across the lough. In 1740, it is said that a hurling match took place
on the lough between teams from the opposing parishes. The freeze
brought with it famine and disease, crops failed and thousands died
or emigrated.

'TOTAL DESTRUCTION IS APPREHENDED'

The onslaught of the potato blight in 1845 arrived later in County
Antrim than it did on the rest of the island. In October 1845, it was
reported in Ballymena that, 'The decay in this district is very general.
Many persons, who thought that their crops were free from taint,
are now ready to acknowledge that they are seriously affected.' It
was reported that 'no species of potato or the kind of soil seems
exempt from the disease ... the rot seems to prevail most in heavy
clay soils, and black seeding potatoes are thought to be most
affected'. However, the crop grown by Lord Massereene in Antrim
had escaped the worst ravages of the blight and he was able to sell

potatoes at market at inflated prices. Alexander Davison, secretary of the Ballymena Agricultural Society, reported on 23 September, that 'there are few fields where the failure has not manifested itself, and particularly in those earliest planted and it is to be feared as the season advances that injury will extend. Nothing that I am aware of has been done to arrest its progress.'

In the north of the county, the Ballycastle Agricultural Society reported that, 'The disease has affected the potato crop in this neighbourhood to a considerable extent. In some parts fears are entertained that one-third of the crop will not be safe.' Such was the total reliance on the potato in the area that it was reported that pigs and cattle had died from feeding on the diseased portion of the potato. William McMaster of Ballycastle reported, 'Latterly the potatoes when taken up appear in many cases free from decay, yet when boiled they are found to be hard and discoloured, very offensive to the smell, and altogether unfit for food.' He added that the prospects looked bleak for the potato crop, adding that failure, 'which I fear will be very prevalent, is frightful to contemplate'.

By 1846, the situation in the county had worsened greatly and, in March, the medical officer for Antrim described the abject condition of the people of Randalstown. His report read, 'Jaundice and diarrhoea exist from the unsoundness and insufficiency of food. The breaking out of disease is apprehended where destitution exists.' Early the following year, prospects seemed to improve. In May 1847, at Belfast's Montgomery Street market, upwards of thirty cartloads of potatoes were sold in one day, indicating that the crop that year would be bountiful. Regardless, *The Vindicator* was to report two months later that, 'The poverty and disease that stalk through the streets of this town [Belfast] have scarcely ever been equalled during the memory of the oldest inhabitant. In every street, on the footpaths and door-steps, are to be seen groups of miserable creatures sitting or lying and apparently suffering from the attacks of hunger and sickness. They stretch themselves in the sun and for hours sleep in that exposed condition, and by this means their physical disorders become more confirmed and increased.' In August, it was reported, 'From Antrim, Tyrone and Donegal, the accounts are the same – everywhere total destruction is apprehended'.

LORD MASSEREENE'S
OPTIMISTIC OUTLOOK

On Friday, 7 November 1845, the captains of industry gathered in a field belonging to James Thompson of Whitehead for a ceremonial event to mark the beginning of extension work on the Belfast-to-Ballymena railway line. The scene was bedecked in flags and bunting and a band played to a crowd of over 1,500 that had gathered to hear the speeches which marked the historic occasion. The chief guest on the day was Lord Massereene, who 'presented himself in the midst of the assembly'. Addressing the crowd, he struck an air of patronising optimism, despite the impending disaster that was the failure of the potato crop:

> The present is a period of very great distress, owing to the failure of the crop which forms a large portion of the poor man's food. A work of this kind [the railway] is therefore so much more needed on that account, as it will be the means of circulating a great amount of money among the labouring classes. They will therefore be more enabled to meet the calamity I have referred to (cheers). We ought to cherish gratitude to Divine Providence for allowing us to meet together and commence an undertaking which will result in so much public benefit; and I trust that the first spade-full of earth turned up this day will eventually produce a plentiful harvest to the shareholders, whilst the first advantages will accrue to those who need it most, the working classes. I'm afraid that a period of very great distress is at hand, during which a work such as that which about to be commenced on would be likely to put as much money into the pocket of the labouring classes of the neighbourhood, and would, in a great measure, counteract the results of the failure of the potato crop. At such a time, they [the labouring class] ought to give great thanks.

POTATO BLIGHT IN BALLYCARRY

While it is generally accepted that County Antrim escaped the worst excesses of the Irish famine during the 1840s, the years 1845 to 1850 were trying years for the county. The growth of Belfast during that period was due, in part, to the migration of thousands of dispossessed peasants from across Ulster to the town. In 1845, the potato crop in Antrim was badly affected by the blight, but not to the extent that people starved. In November that year, Revd John Stuart, Presbyterian minister of Ballycarry, told *The Nation* that, 'in his district, fully one-half the crop is lost', but he believed that his parishioners would be able to preserve what remained of the crop to support them throughout the year. He noted that potatoes on bogland across Antrim had suffered badly from the blight, adding that some districts were was bad as anywhere in the country. Some parishioners had tried covering the crop with lime dust to save what remained and storing them in pits covered with tiles. However, he noted that 'in a few days they [the potatoes] were found to be a mass of rottenness'. Many locals believed that the blight had been sent by God as a punishment. Revd Stuart added, 'As no one knows the disease or the cure, we must resolve all into the displeasure of God, who being forgotten by the people, calls for famine on the land as the seed is rotten under the clods.'

HUNGER AND FAMINE IN BELFAST

At nine o'clock on Friday morning a mob of approximately 200 people, uttering the most foul language, surrounded Mr Bernard Hughes' Bakery in Donegall Street. A number of the ringleaders went into the shop and demanded, 'Give us bread, or we shall take it by force.' Mr Hughes refused stating that he had already given a lot to charity. The men became more violent and passers-by gave them money which they spent on bread. The crowd then went to a bakery in Church Street and demanded bread, and after that went to Mr Smith's bakery in North Street where they were arrested by the police, tried and given the choice of either paying a 20 shilling fine of going to jail for 14 days. The ringleader, Henry Walker, either paid a fine of 40 shillings or spent a month in custody.

(*Belfast News Letter*, 22 December 1846)

'BLACK '47' COMES TO BELFAST

The coming of the Great Famine impacted greatly on Belfast as thousands of people flocked to the town in search of relief. One of the initiatives the government introduced was the setting-up of soup kitchens which served a dish known as 'stirabout', which consisted of porridge, Indian corn meal and rice, cooked with water. Each serving of this potion was accompanied with a 4-ounce slice of bread, but slowly and surely the people starved. In February 1847, the Belfast Relief Committee oversaw the distribution of 21,880 quarts of soup and 7,200lbs of bread to the starving. The cost of providing this support was exorbitant and was paid for mainly through charitable donations. The numbers presenting themselves at the soup kitchens in Belfast rose by 400 persons each week during February 1847. The *Belfast News Letter* reported that the Relief Committee was facing an unprecedented crisis and it had admitted 'that the town is in a state of destitution, more common than is commonly believed'. The *Belfast News Letter* reported the deathly effects of the famine in Belfast in its edition of 20 July 1847:

> It is now a daily occurrence in Belfast to see haggard, sallow and emaciated beings stricken down by fever or debilitated from actual want, stretched prostrate on the footways of our streets and bridges, utterly helpless and unable to proceed from the spot where they have fallen down. In a field on the Old Lodge Road, lay a wretched mother and her fevered boy, with his burning head on a pillow of straw, his legs quivering under a thin blanket, his mother hopeless and helpless, shielding him from the scorching sun. It was not until late evening that the mother was able to get assistance and remove her child to the fever hospital.

Death was a common occurrence in the streets of the town, with most of the victims being buried in communal plots. The 'Plaguey Hill' in Friar's Bush Graveyard in south Belfast contains a memorial stone commemorating 800 victims of the famine in the city. Such was the pressure on the graveyard as a result of the famine that an overflow pit was dug in the Shankill Graveyard.

'SUDDEN DEATHS' IN COUNTY ANTRIM

The Great Famine saw a severe increase in deaths from destitution in Belfast. In May 1847, an unknown man was discovered in a byre belonging to Mr Coates at Malone. The poor soul, aged between 50 and 60, had been turned away from the workhouse in Belfast and had sought refuge in the nearby countryside. Such was his condition, the *Northern Whig* reported, 'that he was unable to utter a word and died within an hour from hunger and want'. Later that day, a man from Ballymoney collapsed at the gates of the night asylum and died before he could be treated. His cause of death was given as 'destitution' by the doctor who arrived at the scene. Given the number of sudden deaths in Belfast at the time, magistrates deemed that there were no need for official inquiries into these deaths and the signing of a death certificate by a physician was sufficient to ensure burial. the *Vindicator* newspaper described such a move by the authorities as 'culpable negligence'.

THE DEFACED FAMINE STONE

Frances Anne Vane (1800–1865), Marchioness of Londonderry, inherited the title of Countess of Antrim, as well as significant lands between Glenarm and Cushendall, which included the coastal town of Carnlough. During the Great Famine, the Londonderry family were pro-active in addressing the suffering of their tenants. They provided assistance for the people of the area and established soup kitchens. In 1847, they established an Estate Relief Committee, which sought to encourage tenants to diversify the crops they grew, organised fundraising events and distributed clothing to the poor. In 1849, the marchioness erected a 'Lettered Stone' on the Antrim Coast at Garron Point, as a memorial to the suffering brought to the area by the potato famine. It reads:

> Francis Anne Vane, Marchioness of Londonderry, being connected with this province with the double ties of birth and marriage and being desirous to hand down to prosperity an imperishable memorial to Ireland's affliction and England's generosity in the years 1846–7, unparalleled in the annals of human suffering, hath engraved this stone:

Fair tablet, fashioned by the Almighty's hand
To guard these confines of sea and land
No longer shalt thou meet the stranger's sight
A polished surface of unmeaning white
But bid him ponder on days of yore
When plague and famine stalked along this shore.
And pale Erin bowed her drooping head,
Like Rachel weeping for her children dead.
Go, tell him, to assuage those pangs and fears,
Britannia gave her bounty with her tears,
And bear this record though in phrases rude,
Of England's love and Ireland's gratitude.

The line within the citation to 'England's generosity in the years 1846–7' was not met with universal endorsement by many in the Glens of Antrim. Soon after its erection, the reference to 'England's generosity' was chipped off by disgruntled locals, as were the final four lines, which recorded, specifically, that 'Britannia gave her bounty with her tears'.

CHOLERA IN BELFAST

It is with deepest regret we have to state that no fewer than twenty-four cases of cholera have occurred in this town since Tuesday last, and that the disease has assumed a very aggravated character, and has proved unusually fatal. Ten of the cases to which we allude have been treated privately, the others at the dispensary. The home of the disease is, as hitherto, in the ill-ventilated and filthy alleys of the town.

(*Ulster Banner*, 18 August 1854)

MISCONDUCT OF MILLWORKERS – MARCH 1860

The growth of Belfast during the industrial revolution attracted many tens of thousands to the town in search of work in its numerous mills and factories. However, needless to say, conditions were poor and the power of the factory owners over employees was absolute and sometimes brutal. Indeed, any perceived breach of contract by employees was dealt with by implementing the full rigours of the law.

In March 1860, four Belfast boys were charged with 'having misconducted themselves in the employment of Messrs. Mitchell, mill owners, and having left without giving the usual notice'. John Rea and Hugh Blayney, both 16, and Patrick Durkin and Thomas Reynolds, both 14, were charged with absconding from their work 'thereby occasioning their employers great loss'. The boys were all found guilty and ordered to pay fines of 20 shillings each, with costs, or to face prison for one month.

In another case that day, Thomas McConnell, a 14-year-old millworker of the York Street Spinning Company, was charged with a similar offence. Thomas Corrigan, the foreman at the mill, proved the charge and said that the prisoner had 'not only gone away himself without giving notice, but had brought away another lad with him'. He added that it was unacceptable that workers could leave the mill without giving adequate notice since, in McConnell's case, the mill had been left two tons short of stock. The judge, Mr Tracey, cautioned McConnell as a lesson to others, but discharged him, pointing out that he had to forfeit any wages still due to him.

PITIFUL DEATH
OF A CHILD IN GLENARM

On Thursday, 13 March 1862, the coroner of County Antrim, John Jellett Esq., had the unenviable task of carrying out an autopsy on the body of a 5-year-old child, Owen Dougherty. The child was the son of a beggar woman named Mary Dougherty, who had been fined 5 shillings for 'drunkenness' the week before the incident, but who had refused to stay at the local workhouse. She took up lodgings with her children in a local pig sty, where Owen was found dead on the morning of 11 March. The local medic, Dr Moore, deemed the boy's cause of death as 'cold and exposure, together with scanty and improper food'. The coroner pleaded with the jury to find a verdict that would permit him to commit Mary Dougherty to prison for manslaughter and allow her surviving children to be handed over to the workhouse.

RAF TO RATHLIN'S RESCUE

The 6-mile stretch of water between Rathlin Island and Ballycastle can prove to be a very treacherous crossing. The island is surrounded by dangerous, fast-moving tides which flood in and out of the narrow neck of the North Channel four times a day. In January 1934, the island's 280 inhabitants were cut off for a three-week period due to storms and a distress call was picked up in Ballycastle declaring that the islanders were experiencing 'famine' conditions. With the island inaccessible by sea, an RAF plane containing a ton of supplies was sent from Aldergrove Airport to relieve the situation. The islanders lit fires of kelp to guide the emergency plane, which landed in a bumpy field merely 200-yards long. The pilot reported that the islanders had run out of food and fuel and parents had forgone rations in order to feed their children. The landing was the first occasion on which a plane had visited the island and the children were afforded a day off school in honour of the event.

9

ALONG COAST AND GLENS

RED BAY CASTLE

The ruins of Red Bay Castle stand above the Red Arch, a tunnel that was cut through the sandstone when the coast road was built in the 1840s. Lying between Waterfoot and Cushendall, it was built on the site of a former Norman motte, which dates from the twelfth century. Originally it was a stronghold of the McQuillan dynasty, but it presently fell into the hands of the McDonnell clan. The castle has withstood many sieges and changed hands several times. In 1565 it was captured and burned by Shane O'Neill.

The first Red Bay Castle was probably built by Walter Bisset in the thirteenth century after he had travelled to Ireland after being banished from Scotland in 1224 for the murder of an uncle. The present remains, however, are from a castle which is believed to have been built on this site by Sir James McDonnell around 1561. In 1604 the castle was restored only to be destroyed by Oliver Cromwell in 1652. When the famous archway at Red Bay was being built as part of the Antrim Coast Road in 1849, a cave was found in which there were parts of six skeletons, along with two bronze axes, a stone axe and two coins, one adorned with Beornwulf, the King of Mercia in the Midlands of England from 823 to 826, and the other with Coelnoth, Archbishop of Canterbury from 833 to 870.

WINSTON CHURCHILL'S
ACT OF KINDNESS

In 1921, Sir Winston Churchill inherited significant land and property in the coastal town of Carnlough, which had originally been in the possession of his great-grandmother, the former Marchioness of Londonderry, Frances Anne Vane Tempest. The marchioness had built the stately Garron Tower, north of Carnlough, which was purchased by the Roman Catholic Church in 1950 and used as a boarding school. In December 1934, Churchill played the part of Father Christmas when he gifted houses to fourteen of his tenants in Herbert Street. The houses, which were described as being 'in fairly good repair', had been built in the 1840s and the act of kindness was greatly appreciated. That year, Churchill had sold the town's famous hotel, the Londonderry Arms Hotel, to the Lyons family and it still operates as a well-known hostelry.

THE NINE GREEN GLENS OF ANTRIM

The nine green glens of Antrim are celebrated in song and folklore. From south to north, they are: Glenarm (the valley of the army), Glencloy (the valley of the sword), Glenarriff (the valley of the ploughman), Glenballyeamon (the town of Eamon's valley), Glenaan (the valley of the burial chambers), Glencorp (the valley of the body or slaughter), Glendun (the valley of the Dun River), Glenshesk (the barren valley) and Glentaisie (Taisie's valley or damp valley).

CARRICK-A-REDE ROPE BRIDGE

A whimsical little fishing rock, connected to the mainland by a flying bridge.

(*Letters Concerning the Northern Coast of the County of Antrim*, William Hamilton, 1817)

Situated on the causeway coast of County Antrim, east of Ballintoy, the Carrick-a-Rede rope bridge has attracted curious visitors for the past 350 years. Not for the faint-hearted, or those who suffer from vertigo, the wooden slat bridge extends almost 80ft to the small rocky outcrop of Carrick-a-Rede (the 'rock of the casting'). It is said to be the only bridge to span the Atlantic Ocean and was erected over a 100ft chasm by local fishermen to trap migrating salmon on their way to spawn in the River Bush and the River Bann. Despite its precarious setting, fishermen, seemingly oblivious to the danger, crossed the bridge up to eighty times a day weighed down by baskets of fish. Until the 1960s, the bridge consisted of 3ft-wide slats with a rope handrail on one side. An enormous net was cast over the side to catch the salmon in the inlet. However, due to the changing migrating patterns of the salmon, the fishery station at the site closed in 2002. Owned by the National Trust, the swaying bridge remains a popular tourist attraction and, weather permitting, is open all year round.

WORTH SEEING,
BUT NOT WORTH GOING TO SEE

The remote location of the Giant's Causeway led to one of the most famous quotations about the natural wonder. Recorded in James Boswell's biography of Samuel Johnson, the well-known English writer, moralist and literary critic Boswell recounts a rather peculiar conversation about the merits of the Causeway as a visitor attraction. The conversation goes as follows:

> He, I know not why, shewed upon all occasions an aversion to go to Ireland, where I proposed to him that we should make a tour.
> JOHNSON: 'It is the last place where I should wish to travel.'
> BOSWELL: 'Should you not like to see Dublin, Sir?'
> JOHNSON: 'No, Sir; Dublin is only a worse capital.'
> BOSWELL: 'Is not the Giant's-Causeway worth seeing?'
> JOHNSON: 'Worth seeing, yes; but not worth going to see.'

(*Life of Johnson* by James Boswell)

FIRE AT GLENARM CASTLE

Glenarm Castle is the seat of one of the most famous Scots-Irish families in Ulster and the Earls of Antrim, who were descended from the McDonnells, Lords of the Isles. On Tuesday, 25 June 1929, much of the magnificent castle was gutted in a fire which was discovered in a bedroom in the early evening. It is said that the blaze began when a servant left a coal fire, which had been lit to keep a featherless parrot warm, unattended in her bedroom. Immediately, a fire engine, which belonged to the estate, was manned but it was hindered by poor equipment and soon the fire was out of control. Fortunately staff were able to remove a considerable quantity of furnishings, old paintings and other valuables, but the fire raged for a full hour before the brigade arrived from Larne. A strong north-east wind swept the flames through the building and at midnight the two top storeys were completely gutted and the ground floor was a furnace of blazing debris.

The castle was rebuilt in the aftermath of the fire but was criticised for a lack of imagination which saw the original Gothic windows replaced with rectangular ones and the baroque hall lose all of its ornate plasterwork. The castle was restored to its former glory under Angela Sykes, a talented artist who married Randal McDonnell, 8th Earl of Antrim in 1934, who painted other rooms with interpretations of family and classical mythologies.

Another fire in 1965 led to the destruction of the servants' wing, with the exception of the kitchen, which was the only room in continuous use since the seventeenth century. The castle stands today as an impressive rectangular pile with four large rectangular towers at each corner. Although it is principally the home of Randal, Viscount Dunluce, son of the 14th Earl of Antrim, his wife Aurora and their family, it is open to the public and its walled garden is considered one of the finest in Ireland.

LINKING ANTRIM TO SCOTLAND

With the implementation of the Act of Union in 1801, plans were mooted to connect Antrim to Scotland by means of an undersea tunnel. During the Victorian period, given the huge leap in engineering capability, it was believed that such a connection would solve forever 'The Irish Question' by joining the two islands on a permanent basis. In May 1857, the *Washington Post* reported that a project to connect the islands would see the 'the land of St. Patrick with that of St. George in close commercial bonds and may serve to make their sons better friends'.

The first serious suggestion originated in 1868. It was the brainchild of the Irish engineer Livingston Macassey, who proposed the construction of a 'submarine tunnel' below the seabed between Torr Head and the Mull of Kintyre in Scotland. Despite the fact that the distance, at 14 miles, was determined to be the shortest between Scotland and Antrim, the plan was deemed impractical as there was no established railway line on the Scottish side. In fact, it would have been necessary to extend the railway from Campbell Town to Loch Fyne on the Scottish side, a distance of over 100 miles, to link the route to the main Glasgow line. The plan never received any serious consideration since the travel time for passengers would have been longer than the established boat routes.

However, the most realistic scheme proposed was by the distinguished civil engineer James Barton, a native of Dundalk, who had been instrumental in the construction of the Severn Tunnel, which ran under the River Severn for a distance of over 2 miles. Barton's proposal was to link Islandmagee with Portobello in Wigtownshire. Its advantage was that the 25-mile route would avoid the north of Beaufort's Dyke and the maximum depth under the sea would have been 600ft. Nonetheless, the proposal was considered too costly and too dangerous. Despite the vast leaps in engineering capability, the project was deemed impossible since there was no accurate geological information to enable engineers to make a feasible proposition. Other concerns were that the sheer work involved would have been on an unprecedented scale and essential work to ventilate the tunnel would have been impossible.

THE GOBBINS CLIFF PATH

The sweeping cliffs at Islandmagee had previously been noted in history as the place where many Catholics had been thrown to their deaths by their Protestant neighbours in 1641. However, the site was to become a renowned tourist destination when the spectacular Gobbins Cliff Path opened in 1902. Soon the remote pathway eclipsed the Giant's Causeway as Antrim's most popular visitor attraction. The extensive cliff walk was created by Wexford-born railway engineer Berkeley Wise, who had originally planned a 3-mile walkway along the spectacular basalt cliffs. The pathway was funded by the Belfast and Northern Counties Railway Company, which sought to attract visitors to the nearby Whitehead railway station. It was truly a remarkable feat of engineering and gave Edwardian tourists a heart-stopping experience as they walked along the pathway, which wound its way around the 250ft-high cliffs. Its famous tubular metal suspension bridge spanned choppy ravines and natural aquaria and was considered to have no parallel in Europe.

Inevitably, despite its popularity, the maintenance of the path soon became a financial burden on the railway company. By the 1930s, Mother Nature had taken her toll and visitor numbers had fallen significantly. The path and its metal infrastructure began to show severe wear and tear, leaving the attraction in a dangerous state. A major landslip in 1951 forced the closure of the path and it was abandoned in the early 1960s. It lay in a ruined state until 2013, when restoration commenced thanks to a project funded by the European Union and the local council. The work enabled the re-erection of bridges and handrails and the construction of a new visitors' centre. The famous tubular bridge was replaced with a replica.

In early 2016, the attraction was forced to close as nature once again took its toll. Storms Abigail and Frank brought heavy rain and winds and a landslip destroyed part of the pathway. There was concern over the future of the attraction as geologists pointed out that such landslides were common on the north Antrim coast; they are caused when sloping areas of soil become saturated with rainfall, lose their structure and break away from underlying rock. The cliff path is accessed by a half-mile steep downhill walk, but extensive work was carried out ensuring that the attraction re-opened in May 2016.

BALLYGALLY CASTLE AND ITS GHOST

Ballycastle Castle is located midway between Larne and Glenarm on the Antrim Coast Road and was erected for James Shaw of Greenock in Scotland. It is probably the best example in Ireland of a Scottish baronial castle and has been transformed into a hotel, which is sympathetic to the castle's seventeenth-century features. One of the quirky original features of the castle was a flowing stream which meandered through the outer hall, providing water for drinking, cooking and washing. Of course, the castle is said to have a resident ghost in the form of James' wife, Lady Isobel Shaw. The story goes that the marriage between James and Isobel soured when she failed to produce a male heir for the Shaw dynasty. However, when rumours surfaced that a female child had been born to Lady Isobel due to a liaison with a local sailor, James had her locked up in a turret overlooking the sea from which she fell to her death. Stories soon spread that James had had his wife murdered and today the ghost of Isobel is said to haunt the corridors of the castle. The turret in which she was imprisoned is today known as the 'Ghost Room'.

DUNSEVERICK CASTLE

This impressive site, situated close to White Park Bay on the Antrim coast, was stormed by the Vikings in 870 and again in 924. It fell into the possession of the O'Cahan (O'Kane) clan, who held it until the expulsion of Gilladuff – the last O'Cahan of Dunseverick – who was implicated in the 1641 rebellion against the English Crown. The castle was destroyed by General Munro and Cromwellian troops during the 1650s. It is said that St Patrick ordained Olcan, Bishop of Armoy, at the castle and blessed a well at Dunseverick for the baptism of local converts to Christianity. The ruins of the castle came under the ownership of the National Trust when the landowner, Jack McCurdy, sold the property. In 1978, the last remaining tower at the castle collapsed into the sea.

THE COUNTY ANTRIM WAR MEMORIAL

The County Antrim War Memorial is located at Monument Road on Knockagh Hill, which has fine panoramic views of Belfast Lough and County Down. The hill stands 938ft above sea and the monument is 110ft high. The landmark is in the form of an obelisk and is a half-size replica of the Wellington Monument in the Phoenix Park. The foundation stone was laid by the Countess of Antrim in 1922 and it had originally been planned that the monument would display the names of all of the men from County Antrim who perished in the Great War. However, given the sheer extent of casualties, this was deemed to be impossible. The monument's inscription owes its origin to the hymn 'O Valiant Hearts' by John S. Arkwright. It reads:

> NOBLY YOU FOUGHT, YOUR KNIGHTLY VIRTUE
> PROVED YOUR MEMORY HALLOWED IN THE LAND
> YOU LOVED.

In February 1937, vandals defaced the memorial and removed twenty-one lead letters from the inscription. The County Surveyor reported to Antrim County Council that the cost of replacing the letters was £12 and recommended that a cottage for a caretaker should be built close to the site to deter further acts of vandalism. In supporting the recommendation, Councillor John Boyd suggested that if the council did not appoint a caretaker, 'something worse might happen'. 'Possibly a bit of dynamite as there are some very bad boys about it [the memorial],' he added. The council adopted the recommendation.

10

CULTURE AND HISTORY GALORE

THE HAMELY TONGUE

The heartlands of mid-Antrim are seen as the traditional linguistic home of the Ulster-Scots dialect. One of the greatest exponents of the 'Hamely Tongue' was the Cullybackey poet Adam Lynn, who was born in the town in 1864 and worked in the town's linen industry. Lynn's poetry was written in the local vernacular and has served to preserve some of the rare words and expressions that form part of local speech. His *Random Rhymes from Cullybackey*, or *Random Rhymes Frae Cullybackey*, was published by W&G Baird in Belfast in 1911 and demonstrated his dynamic and effortless mastery of Ulster-Scots. His work reflected the local rural traditions of Cullybackey, such as the Twelfth of July ('tha twalfth') and mid-Antrim society in the wake of the 1859 revival. Strangely, despite his Ulster-Scots upbringing, his work was sympathetic to the twin cultures of Irish patriotism with the Orange tradition. One of his most famous poems, 'Ireland for Me', illustrated this point:

> Each yin loves dear thir native lan', Despite the heat or cauld,
> Ur whither big, ur whither wee, Ur whither young or auld;
> Ur whither rich, ur whither poor, In it A'll wish tae dee,
> I think nae shame, I'm jist the same, Dear Ireland fur me.

('Ireland for Me', *Random Rhymes*, pp. 146–8)

NEAR TRAGEDY IN A BALLOON

Belfast's Botanic Gardens were the preserve of the cream of Victorian society and one attraction that drew thousands to the gardens was the sport of hot-air ballooning. However, a hot-air balloon launch in the park on 3 July 1865 ended in near disaster as the balloon was caught in a strong gale and carried out along the Antrim coast. All had seemed well as the *Research*, which was carrying six passengers, lifted off in front of 12,000 spectators. However, on reaching the Cave Hill, the balloon was caught by gale-force winds and went out of control as it was blown 'like a feather' along the Antrim coast towards Glenarm. With the prospect of the balloon being lost at sea, four of the passengers in the car decided to jump out from a height of 30ft, breaking legs and ribs in the process. The two remaining passengers, a German by the name of Runge and a Mr Halferty from Belfast, were dragged out to sea towards Scotland, but managed to escape at Glenarriff, both landing in a hedge. Their lucky escape was evident as the remains of the balloon were eventually discovered wrecked on the Isle of Islay off the Scottish coast.

'MAY IRELAND BE THE HITHER END OF YE!'

In the seventeenth and eighteenth centuries, banishment from Rathlin Island to Ireland was the severest form of punishment a landlord could impose on his tenants. The greatest curse for a 'Racheyman' was, 'May Ireland be the hither end of ye!'

GLENGORMLEY MILLIONAIRE

In January 1998, Glengormley schoolgirl Tracey Mackin became one of the youngest lottery millionaires when she picked up £1,055,101 for choosing the six winning numbers. Tracey, a 16-year-old pupil at Our Lady of Mercy School, had originally thought that she had won just £53 for choosing four winning numbers and it wasn't until two days later that she realised she had hit the jackpot. Despite her life-changing win, Tracey returned to school on the day following the presentation of her winnings to sit part of her GCSE computer studies exam.

ANCIENT KINGDOM OF DÁL RIATA

A tract of the modern-day Glens of Antrim was once part of the Gaelic overkingdom of Dál Riata, which stretched across the Irish Sea, taking in western Scotland and the isles. Towards the end of the fifth century, the Gaelic colonisation of Scotland began – indeed, 'Argyle' in Scotland means 'the eastern province of the Gael'. Traditionally, close links had always existed between the peoples of the Mull of Kintyre and Antrim and it is believed that the Irish King Fergus Mór mac Eirc was the first overlord of the Dál Riata. The dynasty went into decline in the eighth century with the re-emergence of the Picts as a force. The kingdom was subjected to a number of devastating Viking raids, but in the mid-ninth century King Kenneth MacAlpin brought the Picts under his rule and established the basis for modern-day Scotland. St Columba founded his monastery on the island of Iona within the area of Dál Riata, so the kingdom was vital in the spread of Christianity and the Gaelic language across northern Britain. The name of the kingdom is preserved in Ballymoney where Dal Riada (Dál Riata) High School is located.

DUNLOY'S MEGALITIC BURIAL CHAMBER

In 1935, archaeologists from the Queen's University of Belfast uncovered the first wholly intact megalithic burial chamber in Ireland. Known as Dooey's Cairn, near Dunloy, the chamber was dated to around 2000–4000 BC and provided a complete record of the burial customs of the period. The leader of the excavation, Mr E. Evans, reported that the tomb contained the remains of three cremated bodies, as well as gifts to the dead, which included beads, arrowheads and knives. Hundreds of bits of pottery were uncovered as well as two finely polished stone axe heads which were capable of cutting a piece of paper. The chamber consisted of a cremation passage, which linked to three pits and is the only one of its type ever found in Ireland. It was named after Andrew Dooey, the owner of the land, whose family granted it to the state in 1975.

ANCIENT PLOUGH FOUND IN BALLYMONEY

A wooden plough found in a bog near Ballymoney was seized by police from the town hall in Ballymoney, where the local council had put it on display. The artefact was discovered in 1958 in a field belonging to Alexander Taylor of Drumlee and was considered to be a rare 'Scottish'-type plough, which was estimated to be 3,000 years old. The plough, which was little more than a bent tree trunk without its metal ploughshare, had been donated to the council by Mr Taylor, but authorities in the Ministry of Finance became concerned that the find had not been reported to the Ulster Museum. Amid protests, RUC officers arrived at the town hall, confiscated the antiquity, brought it to the law courts in Belfast and then placed it in the possession of the museum.

TREASURE TROVE ON THE CAVE HILL

In August 1993, a Shankill Road couple walking on Cave Hill, which overlooks Belfast, uncovered a gold Celtic dress fastener by the side of a newly laid gravel path close to the summit. The fastener, which was 80 per cent Irish gold, was placed in the possession of the Belfast coroner, John Leckey, who deemed the artefact 'treasure trove' and placed it in the keeping of the Ulster Museum. Archaeologists followed up on the find by carrying out a three-day excavation,

concluding that the fastener belonged to the period between 1000 and 700 BC. The fastener is on permanent display in the Early Peoples gallery of the Ulster Museum.

KING WILLIAM IN ANTRIM

One of the most significant moments in Irish history occurred on the afternoon of 14 June 1690, when King William of Orange's fleet dropped anchor off Carrickfergus. From there, William mounted a barge and set foot on Irish soil at the Old Quay below the famous castle. William was greeted in Carrickfergus by a military guard of honour, while people from the surrounding districts turned out in their thousands to cheer their conquering hero. A statue in his memory stands in the shadow of the castle.

To good wishes and warm applause, William mounted his white horse and set off for Belfast, stopping at the Whitehouse on the shores of Belfast Lough, where his commander-in-chief, the Duke of Schomberg, was waiting. In 1690, Belfast consisted of no more than 200 houses on five streets. William entered by its North Gate, which stood where North Street today meets Royal Avenue. A welcoming party of magistrates and burgesses, led by Revd George Walker of Derry, greeted the king and a royal salute rang out from the town's castle. The noise of the salute echoed throughout the Lagan Valley, alerting villagers that the king had arrived. By nightfall, the countryside was ablaze with bonfires.

Prior to leaving Belfast, William and his commanders attended a Sunday service at the Corporation church, which is now St George's in High Street. Fittingly, Revd Robert Royce finished his sermon by quoting Isaiah 43:2, 'When thou passes through the waters, I will be with thee'. On leaving Belfast, the king's army marched towards upper Malone and stopped for refreshments at the junction of the modern-day Lisburn and University roads. That spot is now known as King William Park and is owned and managed by Belfast City Council. From there, the army travelled past Drumbeg and Lambeg to Lisburn Castle.

With the landing of William there were for a time two kings in Ireland, James II and William III. When William left Ireland there was only one undisputed king of Ireland. The Battle of the Boyne, which, given the then use of the Julian calendar, was actually fought on 1 July 1690, occurred sixteen days after King William arrived at Carrickfergus.

IN THE FOOTSTEPS OF KING WILLIAM

After William III's fleeting visit to Carrickfergus in 1690, it took a further 271 years before a reigning monarch visited the town. In falling rain, both Queen Elizabeth II and Prince Philip, accompanied by Prince Charles and Princess Anne, who remained on the yacht, landed at Carrickfergus on board the Royal Yacht *Britannia* on 8 July 1961. It was part of an eleven-date tour which saw the royal couple visit the castle and travel to see factory workers in Newtownabbey to the north of Belfast, Antrim's newest town.

CARRICKFERGUS CASTLE

The picturesque Carrickfergus Castle stands on a rocky basalt outcrop overlooking the entrance to Belfast Lough. Its name is derived from King Fergus, the founder of the Scottish monarchy, who, it is said, was drowned during a storm while taking a drink from a well on the rock (in Irish, it is known as *Carraig Fhearghais*, meaning 'Rock of Fergus').

After the Norman conquest of Ireland in 1171, King Henry II granted Ulster to his general John de Courcey, who, given its strategic location, founded his castle in 1177 on the rock adjacent to the town. In 1760, the castle and the town were captured for five days by the French privateer François Turot as part of the Seven Years' War. However, when Turot realised that the anticipated French invasion of Ireland was stillborn, his fleet sailed out of Belfast Lough where it was intercepted by British ships close to the Isle of Man, where he was killed in the ensuing battle.

Like all ancient castles, Carrickfergus has its own resident ghost, who derives his name from the well from which King Fergus is said to have drunk – Button Cap's Well. The ghost is said to appear on one of the castle's cannons, beating a ghostly drum when turmoil is expected and can be identified by his large hat which is adorned by a huge button. The ghost is purported to be Timothy Lavery, an innocent man who was hanged at the castle in the 1760s.

CARRICKFERGUS CASTLE'S
LAST MILITARY POSTING

In January 1927, the War Office in London abolished Carrickfergus Castle as a military station. It had for decades been the home of the Artillery and Ordnance Corps, which was then transferred to Belfast. The castle had been a constant troop station since Norman times. Today the castle is a well-preserved tourist attraction and is considered one the best examples of its kind in Ireland.

HISTORIC ARTEFACTS
RETAINED IN ANTRIM CASTLE

Algernon William John Clotworthy Skeffington, 12th Viscount Massereene was a devout Unionist at heart. Living in stately opulence in Antrim Castle, he was a direct descendant of John Foster, the last speaker of the Irish House of Commons. With the implementation of the Act of Union in 1801, the Irish House of Commons was abolished and the Massereene family took into its possession the mace and the Speaker's chair of the old parliament. The artefacts were kept in Antrim Castle until 1908, when Viscount Massereene lent them to the Irish National Museum in Kildare Street for display purposes.

With the prospect of Home Rule being implemented in 1914, the viscount took pre-emptive action in December 1913 by repossessing the items from the museum and taking them back to Antrim, lest nationalists would claim them for any newly established Dublin parliament. The mace remained the property of the Massereene family until it was sold at auction at Christie's of London in 1937 to the Bank of Ireland for £3,100. The mace, which contains 295 ounces of pure silver, is displayed in the Bank of Ireland building in Dublin, opposite Trinity College, which is ironic because it is the same the building that was formerly the seat of Irish House of Commons. The chair of the Speaker of the Irish House of Commons is now in the possession of the Royal Dublin Society.

11

A PAST OF TRAGEDY AND DISASTER

NINE MEN LOST IN THE SS *PERIDOT* DISASTER

Forceful gales lashed the Irish Sea on the evening of 26 November 1905, resulting in the wreckage on Islandmagee of the Glasgow steamer SS *Peridot*, which was travelling from Carnlough to Irvine in Scotland with a cargo of limestone. The disaster caused the deaths of the nine men on board, seven of whom came from Carnlough and Glenarm, as the ship was forced onto the rocks at Brown's Bay. The coroner, Dr Mussen, had the unenviable task of holding the inquiry into the disaster. He was told that the crew were seeking shelter in Larne Harbour only for the ship's engine and steering gear to fail, causing it to drift onto the rocks. The loss of the ship and its crew was a tragedy for the village of Carnlough. In 2013, the anchor of the SS *Peridot*, together with a memorial plaque, was unveiled at the harbour in the town.

THE NIGHT OF THE BIG WIND – 6 JANUARY 1839

County Antrim suffered severe damage on the night of Sunday, 6 January 1839, when the British Isles were hit by a tremendous storm, known in folklore as the Night of the Big Wind. The evening began comparatively calmly, but at ten o'clock the county was hit by a violent westerly wind, which soon increased into a full-blown tornado. Thousands of mature trees were lost during the storm, while the 180ft-high chimney at Mulholland's flax mill in Belfast's York Street was blown over, destroying the mill. On the Falls Road, the body of the watchman was discovered amid the ruins of the extensive Ledwich and Dickson linen mill, while in Lodge Lane a husband and wife were killed in their bed when the roof of their house collapsed.

In Carrickfergus, a stack of chimneys fell upon the courthouse, destroying the building, while in Larne six vessels were sunk in the harbour. The destruction at Islandmagee was described as 'universal', with 'scarcely a house having escaped, while numerous stacks of grain have been carried away into the sea'. In Ballymena, six men were crushed to death when a factory chimney at Duvinon's mill collapsed on top of them. More than 300 people were killed across Ireland during the storm, with Belfast suffering very severe damage. It is said that fish from Belfast Lough were found 6 miles inland, such was the severity of the storm. A report in the *Dublin Evening Post* summed up the devastation, 'Every part of Ireland – every field, every town, every village in Ireland has felt its dire effects, from Galway to Dublin, from the Giant's Causeway to Valencia. It has been, we repeat it, the most awful calamity with which a people were afflicted.'

HMS *VIKNOR*'S TRAGIC LOSS

The County Antrim shoreline was to become the final resting ground for many crewmen who were lost in the sinking of the HMS *Viknor*, which struck a German mine on 13 January 1915. The *Viknor*, which was built in Govan in 1888, had been commissioned by the Admiralty for the British war effort in 1914. The merchant navy cruiser was patrolling the seas between Iceland and Scotland when she struck a German mine off Tory Island, near Donegal. The Admiralty had assumed initially that the ship had gone out of radio range; however, bodies soon began to wash up on the Derry and Antrim coastlines.

At Islandmagee and Larne, bodies bearing Royal Marine insignia drifted ashore, while at Rathlin Island the bodies of six sailors were washed up. They are buried in St Thomas' churchyard in two graves which bear the inscription, 'Known only to God'. The remains of Chief-Gunner Kenneth Ballantyne were washed ashore at Ballycastle and he was buried with full military honours in the ancient Bonamargey burying ground. All of the 295 crew were lost in the tragedy. The bodies recovered along the Antrim coast were wearing lifebelts, which indicated that the ship had taken a significant amount of time to go down.

NUTT'S CORNER AIR MISFORTUNE

Northern Ireland's worst air tragedy occurred on 5 January 1953, when twenty-seven people lost their lives in a crash at Nutt's Corner Airport, 14 miles from Belfast. The Viking aeroplane, the *Lord St Vincent*, which had been delayed due to technical problems at RAF Northolt, was due to land at 9.30 p.m., but crashed after circling the airport several times when it struck a landing beacon as it approached the runway. On landing, the plane careered into a brick storehouse and burst into flames. In total, there were thirty-one passengers and four crew on board. Three of the crew, including the captain, were killed. One of the fatalities was Father Patrick Hackett, a native of Augher, County Tyrone, who was returning home from his parish in Devon. Two children died in the crash, one of whom was 18-month-old Francis McCavanagh, who died in the arms of his mother Patricia. Both mother and child were buried together in Belfast's Milltown Cemetery.

TWO KILLED IN GLENAVY PLANE CRASH

A further tragedy occurred in the vicinity of RAF Aldergrove in November 1958 when two pilots in an Air Corps Auster aircraft, Captain Michael Cracknell and Flight Lieutenant George Readman, were killed when their machine crashed into a field at Ballypitmave, near Glenavy. The accident occurred at around 4 p.m. and was witnessed by workmen involved a road construction scheme. One said that the aircraft appeared to be doing turning exercises and that it suddenly dropped into a steep dive and struck the top of a tree. He and other workmen ran to the wreckage but the men were found dead. At the inquest an open verdict was returned by the jury. The coroner had advised the jury to 'accept with caution' any evidence put forward by the 'non-qualified witnesses' (i.e. the workmen) that the aircraft was 'looping the loop' before it crashed.

THE SINKING OF THE
PRINCESS VICTORIA

In January 1953, violent storms lashed the north coast, resulting in the loss of the MV *Princess Victoria*, which was travelling from Stranraer to Larne on the last day of the month. During one of the worst storms in living memory, the ship stalled in the high seas, water flooded onto the car deck and she then toppled into the dark channel and sank off the Copeland Islands near County Down. One hundred and thirty-three lives were lost to the sea that afternoon, including that of the Deputy Prime Minister of Northern Ireland, Maynard Sinclair. Of the 177 passengers and crew on board, only 44 survived. The inquiry into the disaster held British Railways, the operator of the route, responsible for the tragedy, with the reasons stated as badly designed stern doors and inadequate scuppers to deal with the run-off water.

Prime Minister of Northern Ireland, Sir Basil Brooke, summed up the mood when he said that, 'The waves have become a tomb for 133 of our fellow citizens'. The captain of the ship, James Ferguson, remained on board to the end and was one of those who died. David Broadfoot, the radio operator who kept in touch with the ship throughout the emergency, was awarded a George Cross for his actions. The sinking of the *Princess Victoria* impacted greatly on the town of Larne. A distress fund was established and £44,000 was raised for the families of the deceased. A memorial and plaque to the memory of those lost in the incident is situated on the Chaine Memorial Road near Larne.

TRAIN TRAGEDY AT MUCKAMORE

On Saturday, 28 November 1908, people were shocked when news broke that a 2-week-old boy had died after being thrown off an express train travelling between Belfast and Antrim. The incident occurred as the train was passing through Muckamore station and the child was discovered by a William Crawford, who was standing on the platform. Mr Crawford said the child was still in its basket and wore a pink dress and bonnet. At an inquest in Antrim, Dr Scott described how the child had died from massive bleeding to the brain and that 'the force which the basket attained in being thrown was sufficient to cause the injuries'. The jury found that the death was a criminal act on the part of some person or persons. Police enquiries soon led to the arrest of the child's mother, Sarah Ann Reid, who had given birth to the boy on 16 November at the Belfast's Union Workhouse, and her mother Bridget, a resident of the town of Glarryford. At the trial, it was discovered that the child's mother had absconded from the workhouse with the infant on the day of the incident. Both were convicted of wilful murder.

12

BUSINESS, INDUSTRY AND ENGINEERING

OLD BUSHMILLS DISTILLERY

Once, whiskey did not exist, and all the world was sad.
Then came Old Bushmills.

(Old Bushmills advertisement, 1965)

In bygone days, the drinking of illicit whiskey (or, in Irish, '*uisce beatha*' – the water of life) was solely the preserve of the purveyors of the home-made, 'pot still' brand. In Ulster the practice of illegal distilling was widespread, especially in north Antrim. With the advent of the Ulster Plantation and the Scottish taste for 'whisky', regulation of the practice was seen as the best way to control the unlawful trade. Thus, in 1608, King James I granted a licence to Thomas Philips to distil the liquid in the village of Bushmills (*Muileann na Buaise*), which lies 6 miles from Ballycastle on the northern coast.

The origins of Bushmills whiskey can be traced back to 1494 – or even further to 1276. The original 1608 grant makes Bushmills the oldest working distillery in the world. There has been an unbroken history of distilling at the Bushmills site since then and its distinct taste is attributed to two basic elements: locally grown malted barley and peat-filtered water from St Columb's Rill, a tributary of the River Bush, which acts as the distillery's private water supply. The key to its unique taste comes from the malted barley, which is dried and then soaked again in the fresh water. It is then laid on stone flags in the malting shed and dried again over peat fires. The final part of the process involves a delicate, drawn-out triple distillation in the vast

copper stills. It is stored in dark cellars to mature for anything up to twenty years in Spanish oak casks.

Of the three most famous industries of County Antrim – linen, shipbuilding and whiskey distilling – the only one to still survive and thrive today is the last of the three. Owned now by the multinational giant Diageo, Bushmills is a world leader with its three most distinctive brands, Old Bushmills, Black Bush and Bushmills Malt. In 2013, when the G8 Summit took place at the Lough Erne Resort in County Fermanagh, all of the world leaders, including Barack Obama, Vladimir Putin and Angela Merkel, were presented with celebratory bottles of Ireland's most famous whiskey.

FIRST DAY OF THE ULSTER RAILWAY –
14 AUGUST 1839

At seven o'clock on the morning of Monday, 14 August 1839, passengers travelled on the newly built section of railway from Great Victoria Street in Belfast to the Lisburn terminus for the first time. The railway, which had been constructed by the Ulster Railway Company thanks mainly to private sponsorship, ferried inquisitive travellers along the 8-mile journey between the towns throughout the day. The distance of 8 miles was covered in an average of twenty minutes, which included a stop at Dunmurry. It was estimated that 3,000 people made the journey throughout the day, with speeds being described as 'very moderate'. At approximately midday, one of the engines derailed as it was approaching Lisburn station, but 'without causing any inconvenience to the passengers'. The final train left Belfast on time at seven o'clock in the evening, returning at a quarter past eight. By the end of August that year, it was estimated that almost 45,000 passengers had availed of the service. The Ulster Railway Company was taken over by the Great Northern (Ireland) company in 1876. A further station was added at Balmoral in 1858, where the living quarters of the general manager were established (now the King's Head bar). Five further stations opened along the line: Lambeg in 1877, Adelaide in 1897 and Finaghy, Derriaghy and Hilden in 1907.

M1 MOTORWAY OPENED – 10 JULY 1962

Belfast and Lisburn were also chosen as the towns to be connected by Northern Ireland's first motorway, which opened 'to little fanfare' on Tuesday, 10 July 1962. The £3 million route was opened to coincide with the holiday season, thus avoiding any heavy traffic. The 7-mile-long dual carriageway opened at 5.30 a.m. and saw a cavalcade of fourteen cars complete the journey to Lisburn in approximately six minutes. Despite government fears of driving chaos (the government had even published 'Advice on Motorway

Driving' to advise users of safety issues on the new road), the AA reported 'a high degree of lane discipline' and no congestion had occurred at the expected bottlenecks. The first fatalities on the motorway occurred on 12 January 1963, when the cars carrying Mr Herbert Dundas and Miss Hilary Cupples collided. In February that year, the Ministry of Home Affairs issued a statement condemning 'stupid driving' on the motorway, reporting that 883 vehicles had been immobilised during the first six months of the highway's operation. Of those, 251 had been cases of cars running out of petrol.

ANTRIM'S CULINARY DELICACY?

One of County Antrim's best-known exports is the Lough Neagh eel, of which there are thought to be 200 million present in the lough. The eels originate in the Saragossa Sea in the Caribbean and travel with the Gulf Stream to an estuary at the mouth of the River Bann. At Toome, the world-renowned eels are harvested in their tens of thousands. More than 500 tonnes of the delicacy are exported from Toome each year to Billingsgate Market and further to Holland, Germany and the Far East. Together with the Comber potato and Tayto cheese-and-onion potato crisps, eels are synonymous with Northern Ireland food products. However, the eel is a somewhat acquired taste which the modern-day local population do not find to be palatable. There is evidence, though, that eels were central to the diet of Mesolithic people in the Antrim area. In the 1950s, the Northern Ireland government tried in vain to promote the food locally, even promoting the 'Miss Irish Eel' competition. Nutritionists even endorsed the eel as a 'thinning and beauty enhancing diet', which could cure catarrh and liver complaints.

Traditionally, the eel-fishing industry was controlled by a group of English and Dutch merchants, who oversaw the livelihoods of the local fishermen by setting the trading price. In 1963, local priest Father Oliver Kennedy helped to establish the Lough Neagh Fishermen's Co-Operative Society (LNFCS) and hence began a locally inspired process of buying out the London-based consortium. By the early 1970s, the society had acquired sufficient shares to take control of fishing rights. In 2011, in recognition of the 'heritage, tradition and authenticity' value, the Lough Neagh eel was awarded Protected Geographical Indication (PGI status). The award recognised the unique quality of the foodstuff as a world leader. Until quite recently, wriggling Lough Neagh eels were a common site in many pie-and-eel shop windows across London. However, such displays are rare today, but jellied eels are still a popular delicacy in bars across the British Isles, especially in the East End. The biggest commercial wild-eel fishery in Europe is on Lough Neagh in Northern Ireland, a £4-million-a-year operation that employs about 350 fishermen. It produces about 700 tons of eel a year, 100 tons of which is sold in the UK.

SHOTGUNS PRODUCED IN EEL-POACHING WAR

The strict control of eels in Lough Neagh caused an endless game of cat and mouse between poacher and bailiffs. In 1929, Edward O'Neill, a fisherman from Randalstown, was bound over to keep the peace for twelve months when charged with using threatening and abusive language towards Samuel J. Moore, a water bailiff. Moore had challenged O'Neill, who was stealing eels from a tank in Lough Neagh, only to be met with a barrage of 'bad language'. Moore put a cartridge in a shotgun and threatened O'Neill that if he interfered with the tank he would 'blow his brains out'.

In 1966, a 25ft fishing boat sank after being 'intercepted' by a fishery protection vessel in the lough. Two men, who were thought to have been poaching, jumped to safety and swam ashore. The incident took place off Ram's Island, near Crumlin, and was raised at Stormont by Harry Diamond (Republican Labour), who said that he understood a trawler had gone down in a 'naval engagement' in the lough.

In 1967, the persistent eel-poaching problem on Lough Neagh forced the owners of the Eel Fishery Company, in conjunction with fishery protection vessels, to hunt down gangs with a spotter plane. In September of that year the plane was peppered with shotgun pellets as it swooped low over Maghery. The plane, a silver-grey single-screw Auster, landed safely at Aldergrove Airport. The pilot, Ken Malvern, was unhurt but company manager Douglas Barber said the pilot could easily have lost control of the aircraft and crashed, killing him and perhaps others as there are quite a number of houses in the area. There were about sixty pellets embedded in the fuselage on the port side, just behind the cockpit.

AN ENGINEERING TRIUMPH – THE ANTRIM COAST ROAD

In the days before the construction of the Antrim Coast Road, the people and the villages of the Antrim coast were effectively cut off from the rest of Ireland. The east coast of Antrim was accessible only via mountainous routes over the Antrim Plateau. The people of the Glens enjoyed extensive links and trade with Scotland. In the aftermath of the United Irishmen rebellion of 1798, the Commissioner of Public Works in Ireland, who described the area as 'a barren waste, asylum of a miserable and lawless people', established plans to create a scenic coastal route from Larne to Ballycastle. The purpose of the road was both political and economic. Its main aim was to open up trade with the Glens and to subdue any rebellious sentiment that remained there after the 1798 uprising.

The chief engineer for the road, which was originally called the Great Military Way, was a Scotsman named William Bald (1789–1857). Work began in 1832 and it took five years of arduous digging and extensive blasting to establish the first part of the highway from Larne to Cushendun. From there, the road travelled inland to Ballycastle and was completed in 1842, coming in at a total cost of £37,000, 50 per cent more than the original estimate. With the onset of the Great Famine, the road allowed relief to be provided to the isolated communities of the Glens.

The road is considered an epic feat of Victorian engineering and one of the most memorable stretches of road in the world. The novelist William Makepeace Thackeray described it as, 'One of the noble and gallant works of art to be seen in any country'. A memorial to William Bald, and to the men who built the coastal route, can be found inscribed in a humble basalt stone in the round tower at Larne, dedicated to 'the men of the Glynnes'.

HUGUENOTS AND THE LINEN TRADE

During the Ulster Plantation in the seventeenth century, many Scottish and English settlers arrived in County Antrim. They were given government support to encourage them to cultivate the flax plant for local linen production and for use in yarn for export. Much of the expansion of the linen trade in Antrim in the eighteenth century has been credited to Huguenot refugees, particularly Louis Crommellin, who founded a colony in Lisburn in 1698. The French weavers settled in the town and soon began to teach the 'mysteries' of their craft. Crommelin had come to Ireland on the invitation of William III, who was anxious to encourage the industry in place of the wool trade, which had been destroyed by the excessive duties levied on it by English manufacturers.

The linen industry thrived and by the late seventeenth century exports reached nearly 47 million yards. Fifty further Huguenot families joined Crommelin's original settlers and the colony in Ulster soon numbered some 500 persons. The industry thrived with the new skills brought by the Huguenots and, by the beginning of the eighteenth century, Antrim was producing over half of Ireland's exported brown linen. The county was famous for its numerous bleach greens and trade was controlled from Belfast's White Linen Hall, which is the site of Belfast City Hall today. The history of the linen industry in County Antrim is recounted by the Irish Linen Centre in Lisburn.

THE CUSTOMER IS ALWAYS RIGHT

The man behind the creation of the modern-day department store was the Lisburn-born entrepreneur Alexander Turney Stewart. Born in 1803, Stewart spent his early days on the Hertford Estate in the town where his parents lived and worked. His early life though was marked by misfortune as both his parents died when he was still an infant. He was cared for by his grandfather, Thomas Stewart, from Stoneyford, who supported him through his early education at the Lisburn English and Mercantile School. However, while at Trinity College in Dublin, Thomas died suddenly and Alexander, without any means to support himself, was forced to leave Belfast for New York in May 1818. Initially he took a range of teaching jobs in Manhattan. He returned to Lisburn at the age of 21 to collect a legacy of almost £1,000 which he had been left in his grandfather's will. Stewart then decided to return to New York and establish his own mercantile and drapery business. Before leaving Belfast he used his legacy to buy up significant stocks of fancy goods and Irish linen, which he had shipped to a shop he had rented on Broadway. On 2 September 1823, the following announcement appeared in the *Daily Advertiser* in New York:

> NEW YORK DRY GOODS STORE
> A.T. STEWART informs his Friends and the Public that he has taken the Store, No. 283, Broadway, wherein he offers for Sale, Wholesale and Retail, a large assortment of Fresh and Seasonable Goods, consisting of Irish Linens, Lawns, and French Cambric. All these goods were bought for cash, and will be sold on reasonable terms.

Stewart's shop was an astonishing success and he extended his premises along an entire Broadway block. He opened branches in several American cities and sent purchase agents to all the leading European markets to enhance his stock. His retail empire was built on the principle of selling goods just above the wholesale price. He was innovative and held fashion shows and installed full-length mirrors to lure women into his Marble Palace store. In addition, he was instrumental in establishing a lucrative and innovative mail-order business, which enhanced his wealth greatly. He was customer-focused and introduced a spirit of friendliness and confidence between buyer and seller. His business philosophy was based on the principle that 'the customer is always right'. He was probably the first 'floor-walker'; it was his custom to meet customers at the door and conduct them to the proper counter.

He did not, however, forget the land of his birth and in 1847, during the Irish famine, Stewart sent a ship full of supplies to Belfast and it returned filled with migrants, whom he then employed. On his death in 1875, Stewart was considered to be America's third richest person, having accrued a fortune of $160 million. His mansion on Fifth Avenue was of such size and magnificence that it made the nearby Vanderbilt residence look like a 'dilapidated tenement'. His body was to suffer the ultimate ignominy when it was 'kidnapped' two years after his death from the burial ground at St Marks in the Bowery. His distraught wife eventually paid a $25,000 ransom for the return of the body, although it was never verified to be the actual remains of Stewart.

JOHN GETTY MCGEE'S 'ULSTER' OVERCOAT

John Getty McGee's famous 'Ulster' overcoat was by far the most fashionable garment for discerning gentlemen during the late Victorian era. In 1897, the influential *Tatler* suggested that 'no gentleman's wardrobe is complete without an ulster'.

Born in Antrim in 1816, McGee arrived in Belfast and set up a fashionable tailoring business in High Street in 1842. Listed in the town's street directories as 'Tailors, clothiers and general outfitters, woollen drapers, hatters, robe and gown makers, Masonic jewellers, etc.', the firm sought to appeal to a higher class of client.

The premises were later expanded and named the Ulster Overcoat Company in honour of his famous creation. The hefty double-breasted coat, which was made from thick Donegal tweed, together with its pleats, pockets, cape and belt, became a fashion statement and a selling sensation. The 'ulster' brand, sold by the Ulster Overcoat Company, was added to the English language and became synonymous with Conan Doyle's legendary detective Sherlock Holmes. In 'The Adventure of the Blue Carbuncle', published in 1892, Dr Watson records that, 'It was a bitter night, so we drew on our ulsters and wrapped cravats about our throats.' The Victorian era's most infamous criminal, Jack the Ripper, was also depicted wearing McGee's creation in Marie Belloc-Lowndes' 1913 novel, *The Lodger*. In the book, Jack the Ripper stalks the alleys of Whitechapel swathed in an ulster.

The coat is referred to also James Joyce's *Dubliners*. In the chapter 'Grace', we hear of Mr Power, 'a tall agile gentleman of fair complexion, wearing a long yellow ulster, [coming] from the far end of the bar, to assist a Mr. Kernan who had fallen down drunk in the lavatory of a public house'. A lightweight version of this coat was called an 'ulsterette'. The McGee brand went into decline after the First World War, during which it supplied coats to the troops at the front. The firm finally folded in 1940.

WRIGHTBUS AND THE 'BORIS BUS'

Travel anywhere in the United Kingdom on public transport and chances are that you will board a bus made in the Ballymena factory of Wrightbus. Established in 1946, the company was set up by Robert Wright, who began his business by carrying out repairs on the vans of his local Co-operative society. The business grew and began making mobile shops and libraries, flat-bed trailers and, during the Troubles, armoured cars. Its first buses were made for the local education authority in 1955 and then as touring coaches for Irish showbands. In the 1970s, the firm began to win orders for more conventional buses and in 1976 it became a leader in the public service vehicle market. The 1990s saw Wrightbus develop into a primary supplier of buses when it became the industry leader, creating low-floor, accessible buses.

Famously, in 2013, the company won a contract to supply 600 of the new iconic London Routemaster buses. Known as the 'Boris Bus' after mayor Boris Johnson, the London Routemaster bus was a triumph of post-war British engineering. Tourists in London who use the 'hop on, hop off' buses today are likely to board a vehicle manufactured in Ballymena. The Antrim firm's diesel-electric hybrid is a twenty-first-century take on the 1956 design classic. The New Routemaster took poll position in the 2011 'Great' Britain Campaign, with passengers Prince Harry and PM David Cameron hopping aboard for the New York launch of a global promotional event.

ANTRIM COAL MINES

The extensive coal fields of the country Antrim, situated on the sea coast, have been recently let by order of the Court of Chancery and a company is being formed, with a capital suitable to their complete development. The seams are of 9ft in thickness, and of excellent and bituminous quality; they extended over 7,000 acres, and promise a complete supply to the City of Dublin, and to Belfast, Londonderry, Dundalk and the whole north-eastern and western portions of Ireland. The mineral resources of Ireland are now happily beginning to be appreciated; and every well-wisher of the country must desire, as we do, the roost complete success to the enterprise.

(*Freeman's Journal*, 28 January 1840)

DUNLUCE CASTLE AND THE GIANT'S CAUSEWAY TRAM

Trinity College-educated County Antrim brothers William and Anthony Traill invented the world's first hydro-electric tramway. They were responsible for the construction of the Giant's Causeway Tramway. The 3ft narrow-gauge line harnessed hydro-electric power and the first section, linking Bushmills with Portrush, opened on 29 January 1883. The opening took place at Portrush and the line ran for 8 miles along the coast road to Bushmills and onwards to the Giant's Causeway. The official ceremony was performed by Ireland's Lord Lieutenant Lord Spenser in September that year and the 'noiseless smokeless locomotive' was described as 'one of the most unique, scenic attractions in the world'. Initial trade was excellent as passengers queued to pay their sixpences for the picturesque ride. Four years later, a second section connected Bushmills with the Giant's Causeway. The original line closed in 1949 due to reduced passenger numbers and high maintenance costs.

13

MISCELLANEOUS MUSINGS FROM THE NORTH EAST

DAMAGES OF £150 FOR THE LADY WHO WAITED

When Samuel Hill of Crumlin broke off his twenty-one-year-long courtship of Ellen Martin of Carrickfergus, it was a decision that ended up in a protracted legal battle at the County Antrim Assizes in March 1913. The two had met in 1883, when Ellen was 19 and Samuel was 27 and they had been 'an item' until Samuel had emigrated from Antrim to Canada in 1885, leaving his fiancée with a ring and a promise of marriage on his return. Their long-distance courtship lasted for over twenty years until Ellen received a letter from Samuel in 1909, in which he wrote that 'her memory had haunted him' and that he was returning home with the intention of turning a patient fiancée into a blushing bride. On his return, Samuel's affections had cooled somewhat and he began seeing another woman. He bought a house and land and soon walked his new love up the aisle, much to Ellen's displeasure. The scorned woman immediately filed for damages of £1,000 and it was found by the jury that Samuel had indeed breached a promise to his former fiancée. He was fined £150.

UNDERWATER BOXING
IN PORTBALLINTRAE

On Saturday, 25 May 1968, police were called to the sleepy fishing port of Portballintrae to mediate in a dispute which had flared up between members of the Belfast Sub-Aqua Club and frogmen from a French-Belgian expedition. The divers had been exploring the wreck of the *Girona*, which had been part of the Naples Squadron in the Spanish Armada, which sank on 26 October 1588. The ship had struck a basalt outcrop of the Giant's Causeway and sunk with her commander Don Alonso de Leiva and 1,300 soldiers. For nearly 400 years the ship and its contents lay undisturbed until a *National Geographic*-sponsored expedition, led by Robert Steuit, discovered the wreck in 1967. Since then, Steuit and a team of divers had recovered many priceless objects ranging from a cannon and cannon-balls to beautiful gold ornaments and jewels.

The trouble began when a member of the French diving team had tried to prevent one of the Belfast frogmen from lifting an object on the seabed. The Belfast Sub-Aqua Club claimed that their member had been attacked underwater. Robert Steuit insisted that he had merely 'gestured' that the Belfast diver should not lift the object as it was his duty to 'discourage souvenir hunters'. Police were said to be investigating the alleged assault.

ANTRIM OPPOSITION TO
CATHOLIC EMANCIPATION

The prospect of the enactment of the Roman Catholic Relief Act of 1829, in response to the Catholic Emancipation movement led by Daniel O'Connell, was not well received in January that year by the Protestants of the parish of Antrim. On their behalf, a petition was forwarded to the 'Right Honourable the Lords, Spiritual and Temporal of Great Britain and Ireland' imploring them not to support a bill that would give 'political power to the Church of Rome – a Church opposed to the holy and blessed Word of God'.

Requesting that the then prime minister, 'the Noble Duke of Wellington', would stop a plot by the Catholic Church to overthrow Protestantism (a religion created in blood by the holy army of martyrs), they expressed confidence that the bill would be defeated. However, the legislation became law in April of that year, 1829, thus allowing Catholics to take their seats in parliament, thanks largely to the advocacy of the Emancipation Bill by Richard Colley Wesley, 1st Marquis Wellesley, the brother of the 'Noble Duke'.

THE CUSHENDALL GHOST

In January 1935, the villagers of Cushendall were disturbed by reports of the ghost of a woman who was said to haunt the Shore Street end of the village. It was claimed that the woman appeared every twenty years and many local residents claimed to have seen or heard her. She was described as 'a tall figure draped in a black shawl', who was seen hurrying from the beach towards the village and then completely disappearing. Bands of young men, armed with hurling sticks and flash lamps, watched through the night for signs of the ghost. One group claimed to have heard the footsteps of the ghost hurrying past them, but could see nothing. They quickly left the road to the ghost.

THE GHOST OF ETHEL GILLIGAN

The ghost of a young Westmeath servant girl who died in a fire at Antrim Castle in October 1922 is said to haunt the grounds of the estate. Ethel Gilligan, who was 22, died when a fire swept through castle and since then there have been numerous sightings of her ghost, dressed in white, especially by courting couples. The fire is believed to have occurred due to a faulty flue or a defect in the heating system. It broke out when all of the occupants of the house had retired to bed after a house party at about four in the morning. A servant was awoken by smoke entering his room and raised the alarm. Lord and Lady Massereene, with their two children, Lt Col Richardson and some of the other guests hurriedly threw on some clothing and rushed outside.

Cries were heard from a window on the third floor and two maids appeared at a window and shouted for assistance. They were rescued by police with a ladder but it was then discovered that another maid, Ethel Gilligan, was trapped in an adjoining room. When the fire brigade finally reached her she was lying unconscious in bed and by the time she was brought to the ground she had died of asphyxiation. Among the treasures damaged in the fire, the most important was the Speaker's chair of the old Irish House of Commons, which the Lord had taken back from the National Museum in Dublin in 1913. Some furniture and a few pictures had been saved from the drawing room, the library and the lord's study, but otherwise the lord admitted that he had 'lost everything in the world'.

In May 1923, the Belfast judge John Thompson heard evidence in a compensation claim amounting to £90,000 by Viscount Massereene and Ferrard. It was alleged that the fire had been started maliciously and the Attorney General gave evidence that two months before the fire Lady Massereene had received several threatening letters. The judge refused to accept that the fire was anything but accidental. At Antrim Sessions Court in October 1923, a magistrate again refused Viscount Massereene damages to the sum of £60,000 and Lady Massereene was refused compensation of £3,000 for the loss of her clothing. However, the magistrate's decision was most keenly felt by Thomas Gilligan of Castlepollard, County Westmeath, who was refused £1,000 for the loss of his daughter Ethel; her life was deemed to have been worth only one third of the value of Lady Massareene's clothes.

THE OULD LAMMAS FAIR IN SONG

At the 'ould Lammas Fair boys were you ever there
Were you ever at the Fair In Ballycastle-O?
Did you treat your Mary Ann to some Dulse and Yellow Man
At the 'ould Lammas Fair in Ballycastle-O?

The song, which celebrates Ireland's oldest fair, was written by Ballycastle bog oak carver John Henry MacAuley in his Old Curiosity Shop in Ann Street in the town. Born in 1878 in Glenshesk, MacAuley had been disabled in a childhood accident and began trading as carver in Ballycastle. A noted fiddler and souvenir maker, he wrote the song in the early 1920s and its lyrics first appeared in the *Northern Constitution* in October 1925 in a series called 'Songs of the People'. One of MacAuley's most famous carvings was a bog oak table which

he made at the request of the Irish patriot Roger Casement, who sent it
to a friend in the Belgian Congo. MacAuley died in 1937 and a plaque
to his memory was erected over his former shop at 21 Ann Street.

THE GIANT IRISH DEER

Excavations on the County Antrim side of the River Lagan in March 1892 uncovered the skull of a giant Irish deer, which had been preserved for 10,000 years in a peat bog 30ft below the surface. Work had been ongoing in the preparation for the construction of the York Dock near Belfast when the skull was discovered. The animal, which stood 7ft tall at its shoulders and had antlers spanning 10ft, was considered equal in size to the largest specimen ever found, which was displayed at the Kildare Street Museum in Dublin. The nature of the land at the site – boulder clay, fine red sand and peat – was seen as crucial in the preservation of the skull and had been deposited when Ireland was covered by extensive forests. Evidence uncovered in 2009 suggests that the Giant Irish Deer (or Irish elk) had become extinct due to climate change in Ireland 10,000 years ago. With the coming of colder weather and shorter growing periods, it is thought that the deer died out due to starvation. The image of the giant deer has been preserved on the coat of arms of the government of Northern Ireland.

YOUTHFUL ELOPERS
CAPTURED IN QUEENSTOWN

In February 1894, in a tale that could inspire a Hollywood blockbuster, two young lovers from the town of Antrim attempted to flee to the United States because their romance was frowned upon by their parents. Anne Hanney (15) and Richard Johnstone (19), a stable lad on Lord Massereene's estate, had fallen in love and were detained on board the Cunard steamer *Aurania* in Queenstown, County Cork, after a nationwide search.

Miss Hanney's parents had become concerned when her friendship with Johnston had blossomed and decided to send her to a convent school in County Down. Undeterred, the couple, who came from opposite sides of the religious divide, made arrangements to meet up in Belfast. From there, they travelled to Liverpool, where they boarded the ship bound for the United States. However, officials in Liverpool became suspicious when the youthful 'brother and sister' secured steerage-class tickets. When the ship docked in Queenstown, Constables Carson and Clarke from Antrim town detained the couple, who were charged with stealing £12 from Miss Hanney's father. The two were escorted by the police officers by train to Belfast the following morning, where they were met, no doubt, by two sets of very angry parents.

ANTRIM MAN'S QUIET SMOKE

On 20 April 1925, a violent storm caused the thatched roof of one of the oldest houses in the town of Antrim to collapse. Crowds rushed to the house in Church Street, fearing for the lives of two elderly bachelors who lived there, and immediately a frantic search operation began. As the crowds dug with their hands, searching for the men, one of the brothers casually walked down the street and told onlookers he had left the house the previous evening as he feared it would be destroyed in the storm. The search for the other brother grew in intensity as it was feared that he was still within the wreckage. The rescue operation stopped abruptly when a police sergeant arrived at the scene and informed the search party that the missing man was not in the house, but enjoying a 'quiet pipe at the corner of the street'.

Also from The History Press

IRISH DIASPORA

The History Press Ireland